In the pages ahead,
we're going where these were filmed.
These and many more.

The Alabama Hills in California.

Just think of all the movies that were shot here, all the dreams that came to life here.

Filming Roy Rogers' first starring feature, *Under Western Stars*, along Movie Road in the Alabama Hills. Flanking him at the head of the cowboys are Jack Rockwell and Smiley Burnette, Director Joe Kane is in the hat and black topcoat on to of the Republic Pictures camera car. That's a mic' boom extending toward the men.

The Alabama Hills.

They remind you of the Khyber Pass in India. And Texas and Arizona and Utah and Nevada. Even old Mexico and Peru and Argentina. That's because they've played all those parts and more during their 95-year Hollywood career.

Hopalong Cassidy rode these hills, And Tom Mix and John Wayne and Cary Grant and Errol Flynn.

Stare into those rocks and the past is here again...

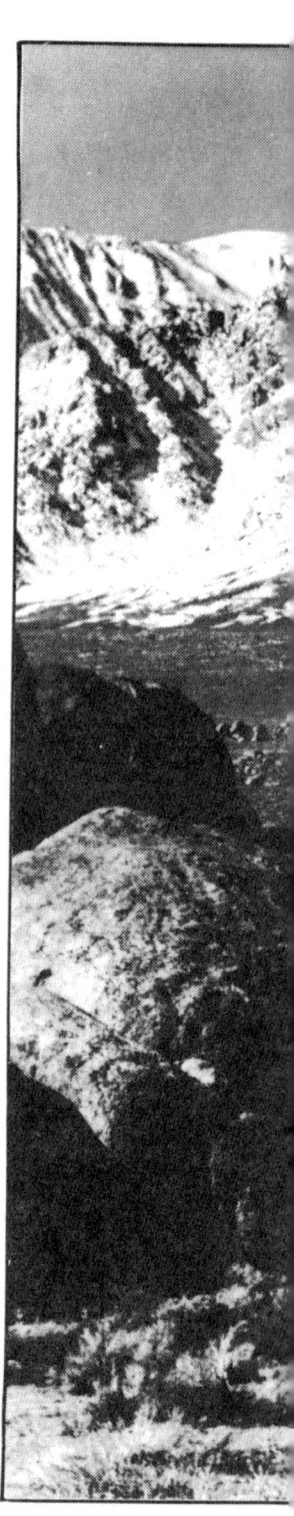

At left, one of the location photos taken to show the RKO executives back in Hollywood where George Stevens wanted to film *Gunga Din*. The two location scouts are in the photo to show proportion. Otherwise, who would believe the size of the rocks? Below, publicity still from the 1939 film.

Filming 1940's *Brigham Young, Frontiersman* out on Movie Flats.

THE HOLLAND HOUSE

presents

"On Location" IN LONE PINE

A PICTORIAL GUIDE
TO MOVIES SHOT IN AND AROUND
CALIFORNIA'S ALABAMA HILLS

by Dave Holland
AUTHOR OF 'FROM OUT OF THE PAST,
A PICTORIAL HISTORY OF THE LONE RANGER'

ON LOCATION
In Lone Pine

A BOOK FROM THE HOLLAND HOUSE

First Printing, September 1990
Revised Edition, July 2005
Multiple printings of both editions since then
Revised Edition, September 2014

All rights reserved.
Copyright 2014 by Melody Holland Ogburn
1990 and 2005 by Dave Holland

This book may not be reproduced in whole or
in part by mimeograph or any other means
(except for review purposes) without permission.
For information, please write THE HOLLAND HOUSE,
16700 Tulsa Street, Granada Hills, CA 91344.

Library of Congress Catalog Card Number 90-093242
ISBN 978-0-692-31465-4

Published in the United States of America.
Designed by Dave Holland, executed by Jim Johnstone.
Drawings by Jim Johnstone and Dave Holland
from photographs (including aerial) by Dave Holland.
Text set in 10-point Clearface 85 type from word
processor discs by Wright Type, Reseda, California.
Printed by Norsal Printing, Chatsworth, California.

DEDICATED
to those who made the memories...

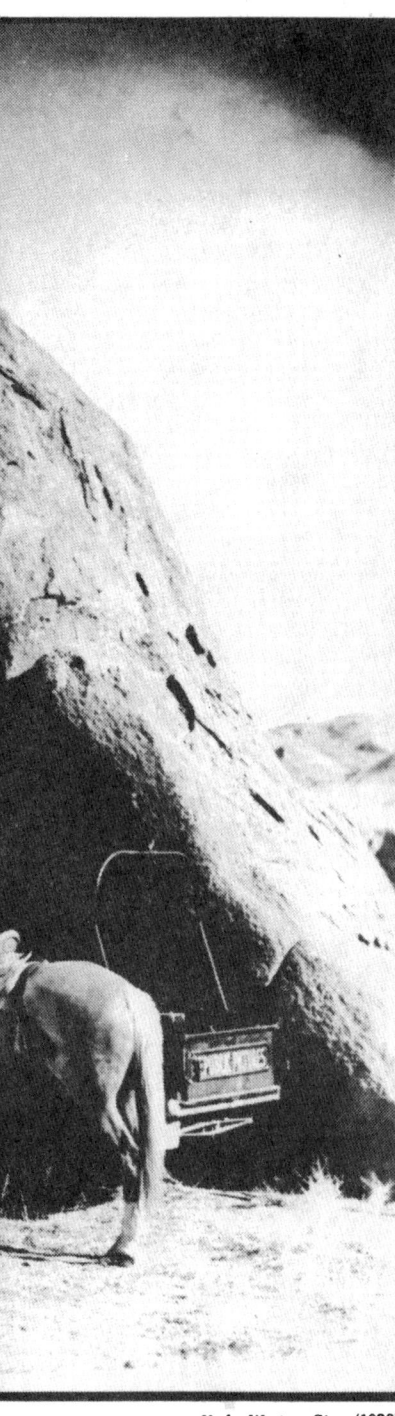

Under Western Stars (1938)

table of contents

preface	10
introduction	13
an overview	16
this man was the movie man	22
area one	32-43
area two	44-53
ruiz hill	54-59
time and time again	60
gunga din - the making of a classic	64
they remember when	74
the 1872 earthquake	76
the stories behind the names	80
go find some yourself	87
and the search goes on	89
the lone pine quiz	99
the author's acknowledgements	105
more to read, more to see	106
gps coordintates chart	107
index	109

preface

Visiting the Gene Autry Rock today.

It was almost 50 years ago now that I first walked these Alabama Hills.

For as long as I can remember, poking around California and the West (looking for the various spots where they made the old movies) has been a favorite pastime, one that has brought about many a glorious morning and many a hot afternoon hiking through rocks and brush at the old movie ranches (Iverson's and Corriganville) and at Hollywood's more "distant" film locations, Red Rock Canyon, Vasquez Rocks, Beale's Cut, Lake Sherwood, Old Tucson, Monument Valley, Oak Creek Canyon, the Alamo Village at Brackettville, Texas, so many more — even Bronson Canyon, which is right in Hollywood! — looking for (and finding) where the Indian chase in *Stagecoach* began, where John Wayne was killed in *The Alamo*, where Audie Murphy held off the Indians in *Apache Rifles*, where the Lone Ranger Rock was and the Nyoka Cliff and Ford Point.

Then one day, I noticed something interesting, no, make that *fascinating*, for it has certainly proved to be that. Looking at a Gene Autry photo from *Boots and Saddles*, I noticed that he and his sidekick, "Frog" (Smiley Burnette), were sitting their horses by a tall, thick cucumber-shaped rock which was — it was so obvious, it was startling — *at the very same spot* where the Indian chase in *How The West Was Won* began and where Tim Holt tried ditching a posse in one of his RKO pictures called *Guns of Hate*! And these were filmed as many as 25 years apart (in 1937, 1962 and 1948, respectively)! I was on the verge of "discovering" a new gold mine of movie locations to go explore!

They were shot, I learned, near a town some 3-4 hours north of Los Angeles — I would later be astonished to learn how many films had been done on location in Lone Pine — more specifically, in that unusual grouping of rocks and canyons called the Alabama Hills, one of Hollywood's favorite locations now for 85 years.

We headed north immediately.

Needless to say, when we first drove out into those Alabama Hills, it was love (and immediate recognition) at first sight. I knew I had been there before, countless times — first in the private darknesses of so many movie theaters, then camped in front of the TV set.

"This is the Khyber Pass," I announced. "I don't care what that sign says, this is the Khyber Pass!"

Hurrying back into the town of Lone Pine, I asked where I could buy a book on all the movies done out in the Alabama Hills, the Hopalong Cassidy movies, the British Army in India movies, the ones with Roy and Gene and John Wayne. "There isn't one," I was told. Well, there is now — and thanks for letting me be the one to enjoy the thrill of the hunt, poring through photos at film conventions and paper conventions and in studio archives, at Eddie Brandt's Saturday Matinee store, at Collectors Bookstore, at Larry Edmunds Books, among others. Thanks for letting me be the one to interview and get to know the townspeople and the movie-makers who worked there.

Now we can all stand where John Wayne stood. And the Lone Ranger and Tom Mix and Randolph Scott.

I hope it was worth the wait.

Dave Holland
Santa Clarita, California
(as written for the 2005 edition)

Where is the Gene Autry Rock? See the *area one* map. And to learn about other scenes from other movies shot at that same spot, see *time and time again*.

Boots and Saddles, 1937.

The Lives of a Bengal Lancer, 1935.

Coincidentally, the "Where's the book on the Alabama Hills?" story is not unique to the author. Other film buffs tell of the same experience when *they* first visited Lone Pine (among them Disney artist Mike Royer and Major in the Tampa, Florida, police department, Ken Taylor).

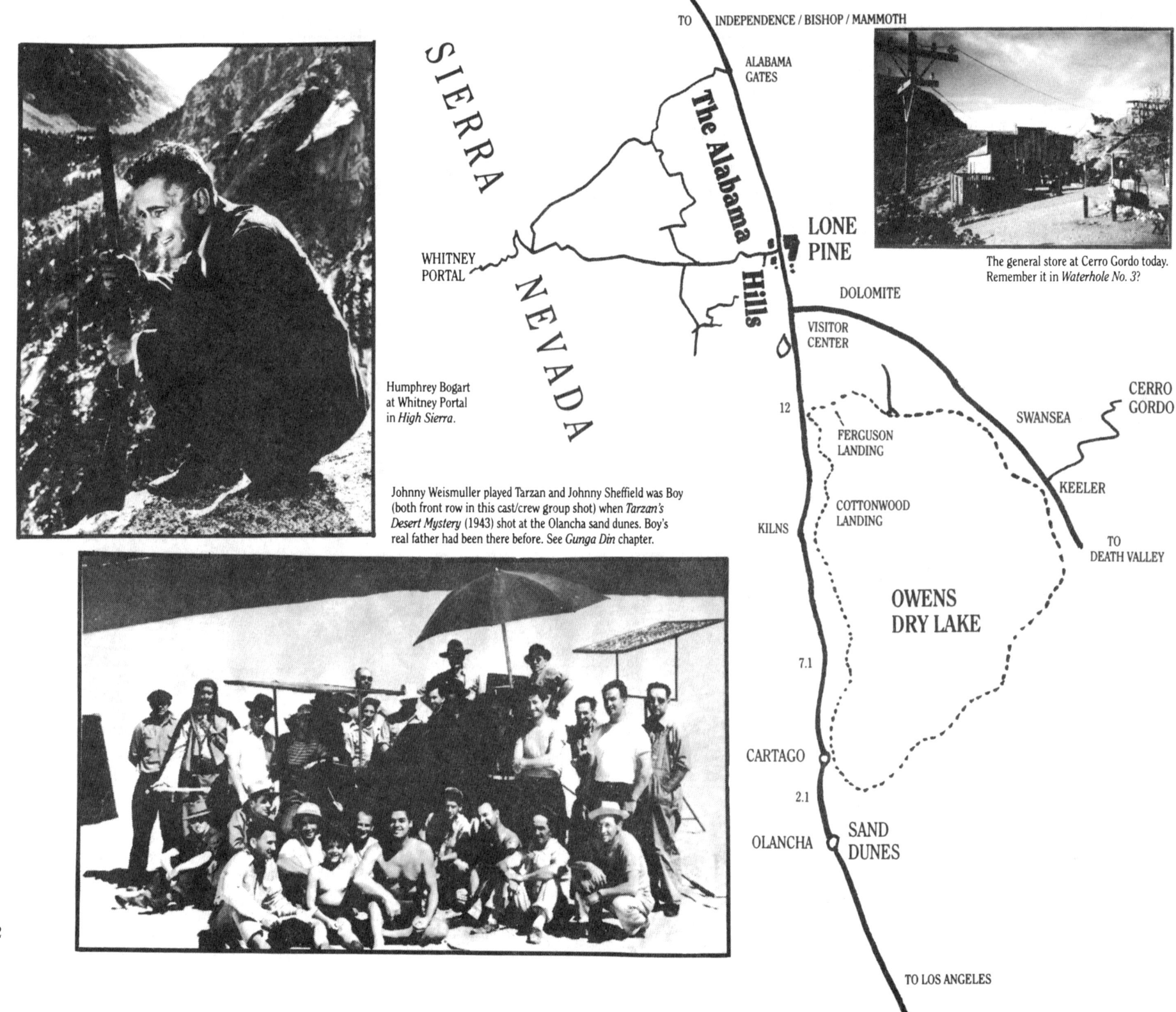

Humphrey Bogart at Whitney Portal in *High Sierra*.

The general store at Cerro Gordo today. Remember it in *Waterhole No. 3*?

Johnny Weismuller played Tarzan and Johnny Sheffield was Boy (both front row in this cast/crew group shot) when *Tarzan's Desert Mystery* (1943) shot at the Olancha sand dunes. Boy's real father had been there before. See *Gunga Din* chapter.

introduction

If you love spectacular scenery and are driving up to Mammoth or Lake Crowley from Los Angeles — going up the eastern side of the Sierras — stop when you get to the desert highway town of Lone Pine, California. Do not continue North but follow Horace Greeley's advice and turn left at the town's only street light. Then you'll be going West toward Mount Whitney... Mount Whitney, the pride of those Sierras, the highest peak in the — but wait. Read what that gas station attendant[1] told Humphrey Bogart in the movie, *High Sierra*...

ATTENDANT

You're lookin' at the pride of the Sierries, brother. Mount Whitney. Highest peak in the United States. 14,501 feet above sea level.[2] Say! I see you have an Illinois license plate! You're a long way from home, aint'cha?

(Bogart looks at him)

You must excuse me. I - I get lonesome here. And when a customer shows up, well, I — maybe I talk too much.

BOGART

Lonesome, eh? Yeah, I can see how you would get lonesome out here.

Lonesome? That's a couple of city fellers talking, men who don't know the desert.[3] Worse than that, a couple of guys who didn't get to the movies much, either. Because how could anyone be lonesome along that stretch of road between Lone Pine and the mountains when there are so many old friends around?

Drive that road and you're cutting through a unique pocket of land that is filled with a host of special memories. Movie memories. Because for 70 years, this has been one of Hollywood's favorite locations, a special place to "go make movies." That's why those rocks look so familiar. You've seen 'em a hundred times, yet maybe never knew where they were.

So stop the car and sit quietly for a moment.

Stare off into those rocks and your mind presses the nostalgia button and the past is here again and the hoofbeats and the voices get louder and you remember that a young boy's heart will break and he'll lose the ranch his Dad left him if Gene Autry and Champion don't win that race. And you can hear Richard Widmark's quiet chuckle as he and Gregory Peck plot to steal Anne Baxter's gold mine...and that baby girl sobbing as Tyrone Power and Jack Elam shoot it out at that stage station in Rawhide Pass...

No, you can't get lonesome with old friends like that around. And you don't. Not here. Not where all those scenes were filmed. Here, on location in Lone Pine.

High Sierra is just one example. Released in 1941, that was the movie which saw the cops chasing Bogart high into the mountains at the end, sending him scrambling up the cliffs to his death.

And when you visit Lone Pine, you can drive the same road Bogart did when he was running for his life. And you can gaze up into the same cliffs where he holed up while the cops and Jerome Cowan and Ida Lupino huddled down below (where you'll be standing) at a place called Whitney Portal (you'll find it on our map.)

Today, it's a campground and jumping-off point for hikers going up to Mount Whitney from the Lone Pine side of the Sierras but in 1941, it was a dead end for that *Dead End* gangster.[4]

And that's what this book is all about: taking you to some of those magical places, standing there together and holding hands with the past.

[1] Actor Spencer Charters. This scene was actually shot at two locations. The angles where you can see the pumps and structures of Ed's Gas Station were shot at a real station which was then down at Little Lake. (It said so on the "location slate" in still photographs in the Warner Brothers files at USC.) But you can't see Mt. Whitney from there so that shot was done along Whitney Portal Road.

[2] It would still be the U.S.'s highest if it weren't for Mt. McKinley (elevation: 20,230; Alaska wasn't a state when *High Sierra* was made, don't forget.) At least, at an official 14,495 feet tall, Whitney is still the tallest in the lower 48 and yes, it *was* listed as 14,501 in 1941 (see the accompanying 1933 map detail). And in *stories behind the names*, you'll read about the people who didn't want to call it "Mount Whitney."

[3] "The desert seems bleak only to the unknowing and the unseeing. It has silence and order and space. It teems with life; you need but know how to look for it." So said Genny Schumacher in *Deepest Valley*, her superb Sierra Club book on the Owens Valley. And anyone who has ever discovered tiny spring flowers in the shade of a sand dune can't help but agree.

[4] Speaking of *Dead End*, even when Leo Gorcey and Huntz Hall and the rest of the guys were starring in their own movies under their new names of the Bowery Boys or the East Side Kids, many moviegoers never called them anything but the Dead End Kids since the Kids were first seen in 1937's *Dead End* with Humphrey Bogart.

where you're going once you're there

Trees still mark the site of the Mormon settlement built out on Hogback Road for Fox's *Brigham Young, Frontiersman* (1940)

That bundle Tom Mix is leaning over in this scene from *Riders of the Purple Sage*? Four outlaws he's just hog-tied at what is now the Lone Pine Campground. Also here were the flume set in *North To Alaska* and Henry Fonda's cabin in *How The West Was Won*.

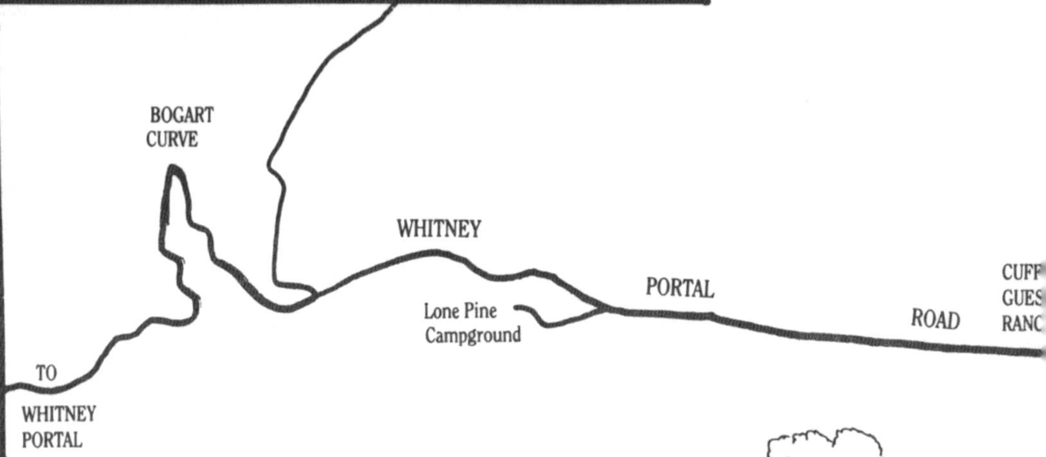

It's called the 'Hoppy Cabin' even today because William Boyd lived in it when he was making some of the Hopalong Cassidy Westerns. During World War II, it was the Lone Pine Country Club, an idea soon abandoned as too frivolous for the times. The distinctive railroad tie construction might look familiar since the cabin's been used in many a film (see *time and time again*).

THE HOPPY CABIN

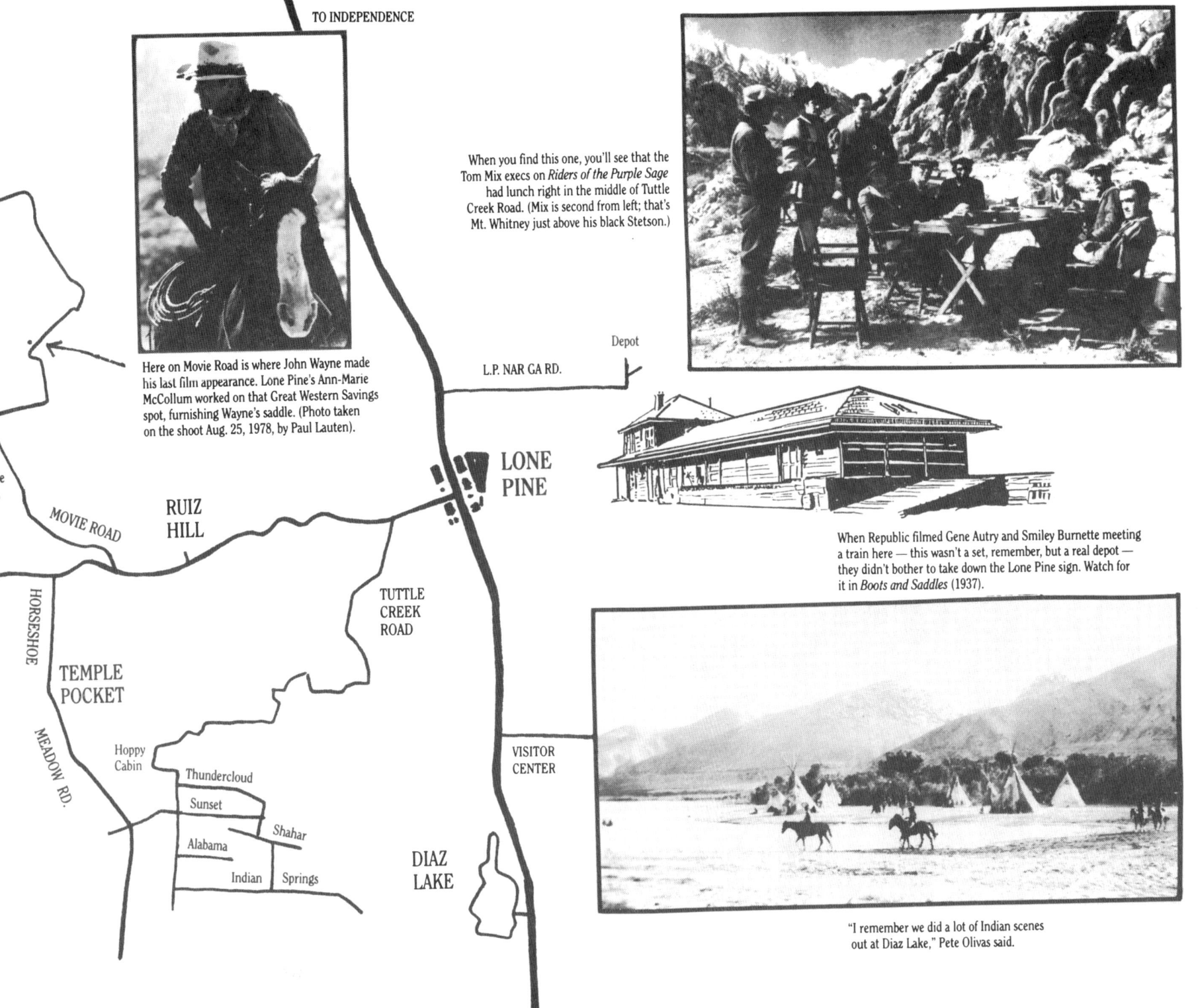

Here on Movie Road is where John Wayne made his last film appearance. Lone Pine's Ann-Marie McCollum worked on that Great Western Savings spot, furnishing Wayne's saddle. (Photo taken on the shoot Aug. 25, 1978, by Paul Lauten).

When you find this one, you'll see that the Tom Mix execs on *Riders of the Purple Sage* had lunch right in the middle of Tuttle Creek Road. (Mix is second from left; that's Mt. Whitney just above his black Stetson.)

When Republic filmed Gene Autry and Smiley Burnette meeting a train here — this wasn't a set, remember, but a real depot — they didn't bother to take down the Lone Pine sign. Watch for it in *Boots and Saddles* (1937).

"I remember we did a lot of Indian scenes out at Diaz Lake," Pete Olivas said.

Tyrone Power leads his men up Whitney Portal Road in *King of the Khyber Rifles*.

Cary Grant in *Gunga Din*.

an overview

Seeing where some of your favorite movies were made in Lone Pine is as easy as looking at maps and photos and looking out the car window. And when you find one location, you'll generally find others, either along the way or often at the same spot (see *time and time again*).

Case in point: When you drive up the switchbacks of the Bogart road — it's really called Whitney Portal Road — you're not merely where the cops chased Bogart, you're on the same road Lucy and Desi almost slid off in *The Long Long Trailer*, the same road Tyrone Power led his troops up in *King of the Khyber Rifles* and the same road Dean Jagger stumbled across in *Brigham Young* to look out over the Owens Valley toward the dry Owens Lake bed and say "Looks like Salt Lake City to me..." (or something like that).

But getting up to those cliffs may not be as easy as it sounds. Not because the road isn't paved or anything — in fact, it's about the only road that *is* paved between the town and the mountains (along with Horseshoe Meadow and Tuttle Creek Roads and some residential streets). The trick is getting past what lies *between* the town and the mountains.

To reach the Sierras, you have to get past the real "star" of Lone Pine, a magnificent maze of eroded and tangled rocks and boulders called the Alabama Hills. They stretch from here to way over there and getting past them is like asking a paper-clip to get past a magnet.

the alabama hills

Just think of all the movies that were shot here, all the dreams that came to life here.

Your own perception of these magnificent rock formations depends on how and when you were first introduced to them.

If as a kid, you went to the movies on Saturday afternoons for a dime at that little neighborhood theater over by the cleaners or were a baby boomer kid raised on Saturday morning TV then these rugged rocks and narrow passes were the scene of so many of the great cowboy adventures with Hopalong Cassidy and Gene Autry and Roy Rogers. And Tom Mix and Ken Maynard and Buck Jones. And *The Lone Ranger* and *Annie Oakley* and *Have Gun Will Travel*.

On the other hand, if you were a little older and went to the movies on Saturday nights down town, then the Alabama Hills weren't associated with the cowboy heroes at all. Instead you remember the "A" pictures: Gregory Peck as *The Gunfighter* or Clint Eastwood as *Joe Kidd* or Kirk Douglas in his first Western, *Along The Great Divide*.

But of all the big pictures done up here, it was probably the dusty images of the British Army on patrol that branded this magnificent rocky setting more indelibly in our minds than any others. Because let's face it, as far as Hollywood was concerned, the Alabama Hills looked more like India than India did. This was the Khyber Pass.

preserving the empire

For years, these sprawling boulders were Hollywood's perennial substitute for India's rugged Northwest Frontier. From the mid-thirties into the '50s if it was about the British Army preserving the Empire, they shot it at Lone Pine and we believed every dusty second of it. Even today, when you hike through the Alabama, you half expect to hear a distant bag-pipe or bugle... that's how vivid the memories are.

At the head of the column, sitting ram-rod straight in the saddle, is Errol Flynn or Gary Cooper. Or Cary Grant and Victor McLaglen and Douglas Fairbanks Jr. Behind them the eager junior officers, David Niven or Franchot Tone or Patric Knowles, always so anxious, so impulsive. But who could blame these gallant young men? This was, after all, the land of Kipling, the land of the Bengal Lancers and the Khyber Rifles, the land of adventure and romance and danger. They believed it, we believed it. Arid for a detailed look behind-the-scenes at Lone Pine's hallmark British Army film, see *gunga din — the making of a classic*.

the names remain

The Movies so influenced the Lone Pine area that even today's place names reflect Hollywood's presence from so long ago.

Not quite three miles west of that traffic light, that road turning off north into the rocks is officially called Movie Road. It was kept the flattest and smoothest by the film companies all those years for use as an "insert road" — which means this:

Say you have a long shot of Roy Rogers dashing along on Trigger but you want to cut to a close-up occasionally (to show that it's really Roy riding so that and so dangerously and not his long-time stunt double, Joe Yrigoyen)

[1] the days when double features were so popular at the movies, the theater-owners logged them in like this: DATE: April 6-8, 19-fortysomething: TWO FILMS: a. *High Sierra*, b: *Cobra Woman*. The "A" film was the big-budget star vehicle while the second feature, the "b" picture, was the less expensive film — not only less expensive to *make* but more importantly, less expensive for the exhibitor to *rent* from the studios. But that a-b designation is how so many of the adventure films and Westerns and comedies came to be grouped generically "B" Pictures.

[2] Two notable exceptions were John Fords *Wee Willie Winkie* with Shirley Temple, shot at the Iverson Movie Ranch in Chatsworth Calif. and 1951's *Soldiers Three* with David Niven, Stewart Granger and Walter Pigeon, shot at Corriganville.

This was the Khyber Pass!

Errol Flynn in *Charge Of The Light Brigade*.

This town was just off Whitney Portal Road

That close-up will be *inserted* into the long shot and to get that shot, the camera obviously needs to be closer so special insert roads were built which allowed the heavily weighted camera cars (sometimes called insert cars) to drive along just as fast but twice as smoothly and film the horses or wagons running alongside.

More? Locals still call that whole area west of Movie Road "Movie Flats."

And on the east side of Movie Road is a certain narrow road twisting through the rocks called "Lone Ranger Canyon." And since Indian actor Chief Thundercloud played Tonto in the Republic serials about the masked man, there's a "Thundercloud Lane" in the Alabama Hills residential area (go South on Horseshoe Meadow Road and left on Sunset).

Then there's Gene Autry Rock and Gary Cooper Rock and the Background Rocks and the Lone Ranger Ambush Site. Not to mention Bogart Curve and Bengal Curve. You'll know them all before we're through.

Meanwhile, back on Whitney Portal Road, that whole S-curve area where the road dips down to cross Lone Pine Creek just west of the Movie Road turn-off is called "Red Dog" because of what went on there 60 years ago!

For a big 1930 Technicolor musical-western with John Boles called *Song of the West*, Warner Brothers built a rather large town on those still-bare flats north of the road just west of the crossing. There was a Red Dog Saloon in town — the town itself may have been called Red Dog, too — and the buildings remained in place for so long afterwards, the name stuck — to this day!

sets 'still in use'

Usually, movie companies took down their sets as soon as filming was completed, selling or giving away the debris, much to the delight of Lone Pine residents.

Dr. and Mrs. George Shultz used the wood from the *Rawhide* stage station (Fox 1951) to build a cabin along Lone Pine Creek. Lumber from the *Yellow Sky* house and barn (Fox 1948) did double duty: it went into a new home for the Clarence Christenson family and a cabin for Don and Alice Homer. Paramount turned over its *Star Trek V* sets to Jodi Stewart and Mike Patterson to use renovating the old mining town of Cerro Gordo. And when *Gunga Din*'s big native village of Tantrapur set was taken down in 1938, Russ Spainhower trucked remnants of that to his Anchor Ranch at the southern edge of town on 395 and began building the only permanent set Lone Pine had for years, a mission/hacienda/ranch house complex.

Courtesy of the Eastern California Museum, Allan W. Ramsay Collection.

Courtesy of the Eastern California Museum, Allan W. Ramsay Collection.

The movie town of Red Dog — just built at far left, abandoned at bottom left — stood for so long, it gave its name to the area. They're shooting the film it was in here and you can see the red Irish Setter sign over the Red Dog Saloon down the left side of the street, thus the name. Below is the permanent hacienda set that was on Russ Spainhower's Anchor Ranch. How often Tim and Chito rode in that far gate! And there are Lucky and Hoppy (Russell Hayden and William Boyd) coming out the *near* gate in *Law of the Pampas* (1939). Note how minor changes were made in the wall height and/or main facade for different films.

THEY DID GO TO A LOT OF TROUBLE

Many thought the old town in 1955's *Bad Day at Black Rock* (with Spencer Tracy and Robert Ryan, left) was really the outskirts of Lone Pine but MGM *built* it out LP Nar Ga Road (which I thought was an Indian name until someone told me that since it once led to the narrow gauge railroad tracks, it was an abbreviation of Lone Pine Narrow Gauge).) The big two story saloon below was not a real Lone Pine building, either, but a set Fox built for Tom Mix's *Riders of the Purple Sage*. And see the little white building at the end of Willow Street? See next page.

the man on the anchor

You can't tell the story of The Movies in Lone Pine without considerable mention of Russ Spainhower. For years, he was *THE* contact man in Lone Pine for the studios.

Paramount, RKO, Warner Brothers, 20th Century-Fox, Republic, MGM, Columbia, Universal — at one point or another, they all called to say, "We're coming up in October. Can you get 75-to-100 horses for a stampede across the flats?" or "Find us a deep canyon with a narrow entrance for the crooks' hideout" or...

"The studios really depended on him" is the proud recall of Spainhower's daughter, Joy Anderson, who still lives with husband Earl on the Anchor. "They got to know him over the years and they trusted him." (See *this man was the movie man*)

When and how did Russ Spainhower first hook up with The Movies? "You saw those snapshots in the scrapbook of Fatty Arbuckle working on *The Roundup*," Mrs. Anderson said. "I don't know who would have taken those but my dad, which means he was actually on the set — doing no-telling-what but *there*, nevertheless — when the movies first came to Lone Pine!"

the first filming

To highlight the added historical significance of *The Roundup*, it is generally accepted that this was the first film made in Lone Pine.[3] Those scrapbook snapshots are dated January, 1920.

In those early days, it was hard to avoid The Movies in Lone Pine. Some of the companies would film "town scenes" right out on Main Street or on the side streets. The bank looked like a bank so they filmed bank robberies there. Other companies (like Fox for its 1925 Tom Mix adventure, *Riders of the Purple Sage*) would actually *cover* real buildings with their own facades or put up false front buildings right in the middle of a street if that's what would look best.

Continued on page 23

Courtesy of the Academy of Motion Picture Arts and Sciences.

[3] And perhaps it was but there is one dark horse contender for that honor. Irene Cuffe, the former actress who runs the Cuffe Guest Ranch of Movie Fame out on Whitney Portal Road, tells this story: Movie director Clarence Badger, who made 1930's *No, No, Nanette* and such silent films as *Miss Brewster's Millions*, *The Rainmaker* and *The Shooting of Dan McGrew*, originally built the ranch on Lone Pine Creek as a hunting and fishing retreat and had such guests as Douglas Fairbanks (Sr.) and Mabel Normand. Badger loved the area and when he directed Will Rogers in *Water, Water Everywhere*, in 1919, Mrs. Cuffe says he shot some exteriors here. (Rogers filmographies list Mojave and the Kern River area as locations but not Lone Pine and a print doesn't seem to be available for a viewing check.)

Courtesy of the Academy of Motion Picture Arts and Sciences.

WHEN TOWNSPEOPLE saw the photo of the white one-story courthouse used in Tom Mix's 'Riders of the Purple Sage,' no one could remember it in town. ("Must have been before my time," Della Cederburg said. "But you see that house right behind it? That's where I live now.")

A search of the archives of the Eastern California Museum in Independence revealed why no one remembered the unique building.

There was a photo showing it was just a false front built at the end of Willow Street. You can see right through it.

Continuing counter-clockwise are three photos of 'The Roundup' being shot (probably the first movie done here). Right from the beginning, film companies used the streets of Lone Pine. (You'll find that exterior location on Tuttle Creek Road, just around the corner from the Hoppy cabin.)

this man
was the movie man

Russ Spainhower

The Anchorville Street

"The movies needed a man they could call day or night, someone who could solve whatever problems they had and make whatever arrangements they needed and my dad just filled the bill better than anyone else up here!"

So says Joy Anderson, speaking of her father, Russ Spainhower, Hollywood's contact man in Lone Pine for so many years.

"He knew the country, he could find them the locations they needed, he could get them however many horses they needed. Or Cattle, Or wagons." Yes, he knew his rolling stock, too. If they needed buckboards on Thursday freight wagons on Friday and Conestogas on Monday, they'd be there.

In the beginning, a rancher named AJ Gallaher furnished horses and cattle for the Westerns. Mrs. Anderson said, but when he moved his stock to Calistoga in the early '30s, Spainhower quickly filled the void.[1] But he was involved long before that.

A native of North Carolina, he had come to Lone Pine in 1909 via Southern California to work for the Los Angeles Department of Water and Power. (Farming was already diminishing as an industry here, that had begun when the City of Los Angeles needed water for its growing metropolis and began buying the 80 percent of the property and water rights it now controls in the Owens Valley).

By the '20s, Spainhower had a ranch the studios could use right in town, not only as a location but as a place to keep whatever animals they brought up themselves "from down below".

He was not only foreman of the DWP he owned Lucas Ranch but had begun leasing it "so he really had something to say about its operation," Mrs. Anderson said. "And I'm sure that, in the beginning, that ranch was a contributing factor to his becoming the contact man up here. His involvement really just evolved."

He rented them the ranch, then found them livestock, then helped them find locations. Soon the word was out: If you were going on location in Lone Pine, Russ Spainhower was the man who could help you, whether you used his ranch or not. "It really grew like Topsy," his daughter said. "He started off doing a little and ended up doing a lot."

His Lucas Ranch had some large corrals and barns, all in excellent condition, all available for use. And use them they did. As early as 1922, Fox shot part of *Just Tony* with Tom Mix in the Lucas corrals and by 1926, there was a special barn for Ken Maynard's horse, "Tarzan," and Tarzan's doubles, five in all.

By the '30s, Spainhower had begun buying cattle of his own, stocking the adjoining rangeland which he bought from Dave Holland[2] and named the "Anchor Ranch".[3] As noted elsewhere, he began building the mission/hacienda set in 1938 but "we didn't move onto the Anchor until 1940," Mrs. Anderson recalled.

Probably the first movies to use the new set were two 1939 Hopalong Cassidy Westerns, R*ange War* and *Law of the Pampas,* followed by *Wagons Westward* (Republic 1940) with Chester Morris (who later was "Boston Blackie" for Columbia).[4]

The last picture Russ Spainhower worked on was *From Hell To Texas* with Don Murray. "Henry Hathaway[5] really wanted him on that."

Mrs. Anderson remembered quietly. "That was 1957, the year he died."

So many years so many films, so many friendships. When Randolph Scott retired, he paid the Spainhower family to let his horse live out his days comfortably here on the Anchor Ranch.

In 1947, Russ added a Western street to the hacienda set – he, the lumber yard's Rudy Henderson and Hopalong Cassidy Productions went in on thirds; they called their movie town "Anchorville."

That street is gone now, so is the hacienda set – their usefulness long over, they were finally torn down in 1975 to make room for a new "real life" ranch house, although the Andersons left some of the old stucco movie wall standing just off the front yard. At least, that's still there. That and the memories.

In 1964, a written tribute to Russ Spainhower said in part:

"His opinion and judgement were highly respected by the movie directors and his friendship treasured."

That says it all.

John Wayne (hatless) with his Singing Riders in *Westward Ho*.

[1] "Now you must understand," Mrs. Anderson said, "my dad was primarily a rancher and he would just make arrangement for the studios. He didn't always rent out his own stock, either; he'd get horses from some of the local packers and rent those to The Movies. That way, everyone benefited." "Generally," Roy Cline agreed "packers would rent their horses to Spainhower and he'd negotiate with the studios, And sometimes he'd let 'em rent direct. For instance, Wilford Cline furnished the cattle and horses on *Springfield Rifle*." "My brother Henry had some 50 head of horses for his pack business," Pete Olivas said, "and some times Russ'd let him rent direct. Back then, they just wanted bay horses or black. Other packers he used through the years were Chrysler and Cook, Allie Robbs up in Independence, various cowmen and ranchers..."

[2] No relation to the author of this book – but no wonder I've been drawn to this country all these years! And if you don't think it's an eerie feeling to stand at Mr. Holland's grave in the Lone Pine Cemetery – (this is the "new" cemetery across 395 from the mass earthquake victims grave at the north edge of town.)

[3] The "Anchor" name originated in his wife's family. The original settler of what became the "Anchor," by the way, was Reuben Van Dyke (1827-1898), whose grave you can see in Lone Pine's *pioneer* cemetery, located .7 miles east of 395 on Inyo Street (marked "Dump Site").

[4] Buck Jones was also in *Wagons Westward* but not in the portions filmed in Lone Pine. He had, of course, shot several things in Lone Pine previously.

[5] Hathaway also directed parts or all of the exteriors for *Lives of a Bengal Lancer, Brigham Young, Rawhide, North To Alaska, How The West Was Won* and *Nevada Smith* in the Lone Pine area.

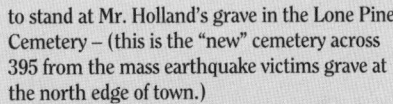

Continued from page 20

So there would be a lot to talk about at dinner — particularly if Dad or Brother did what so many of the young rancher-cowboys in and around Southern Inyo County did on those early cowboy pictures: they signed themselves (and their horses) on as background extras. And why not? It paid five dollars a day!

"And you earned it, I'll tell you," laughed Roy Cline of Bishop, who would later play one of John Wayne's vigilante "Singing Riders" in 1935's *Westward Ho* (they were the ones who wore white scarves and rode white horses so they would be quickly identified in a big fight with the "bad guys.")

"In the beginning," Cline told me, "they didn't haul the horses out, you'd ride 'em out. Ride one and lead six."

Henry Olivas — everyone called him "Leakey" — remembered it that way, too. "There were no paid wranglers in those days," he once told the Lone Pine Chamber of Commerce when it began preserving memories of the "movie days."

"After breakfast," he said, "you had to go to the corral, catch your own horse, saddle him and ride to location. You worked all day, rode back at night and then took care of your own horse. No hired wranglers to do this for you (like nowadays)."

"And you really did it all for five dollars," Cline said. "You did a fall or rode or played one of the good guys *and* one of the bad guys,[4] it didn't matter, it was everything for five dollars, sun-up to sundown. So 17 of us formed the Inyo Riders Association and got a raise to $7.50. Then, when the Actors' Guild came in,[5] it went to $11 for eight hours." And he laughed again.

"(You) did whatever there was to do," Henry Olivas said. "Wrangling, packing, be an Indian, I did it all. Sometimes I drove a dump truck or the water truck," he continued.

"When we did *Army Girl*,[6]" Cline said, "there was one scene where we had to slide down those sand bluffs east of Lone Pine on our horses[7] so they greased up some two-by-twelves and put 'em just under the dirt so the horses would slide better.

"In another shot in that picture," he went on, "one of our riders was a fella named Hardrock Jim. He wore these big thick glasses, couldn't see a thing without 'em and naturally, they didn't want him wearin' the glasses on camera so here we are, racin' along with this Injun chasin' us right toward a four-inch cottonwood tree. That's where Hardrock and his horse parted company." Cline couldn't help laughing. "That night," he grinned, "he took his axe and went out there and took that thing down."

Even into the '50s, townspeople signed up as extras. "'Bout all you had to do was show up to be in a crowd scene," Rellis Amick said. "On *Brigham Young*, I think half the town was down there for the river shots. And they almost roasted. Everybody was bundled up like it was winter and it was a 100 in the shade!"

good guys do wear black

Whether being chased or doing the chasing, the good guys in the white hats were a Hollywood staple for years and certainly a familiar sight in the Alabama Hills. But there was one good guy in a black hat.

Indeed, if there's one cowboy hero who's identified with the Alabama Hills — and vice versa — it's Hopalong Cassidy. Just as all those Republic Westerns and serials showcased the Iverson's location ranch in Chatsworth, California, so did the Hoppys showcase the Alabama Hills.

If Lone Pine was the Khyber Pass to Mom and Dad, to us kids it was Texas or Old Mexico or Argentina. (In *Law of the Pampas*, this was Argentina!) In other words, it was wherever Hoppy said it was.

William Boyd played Hopalong Cassidy in 66 theatrical features — still a record[8] — between 1935 and 1948 and more than a third of them were shot in Lone Pine, including the first one, *Hop-A-Long Cassidy*.

Clarence E. Mulford wrote his first Bar 20 ranch stories in 1904 (published in *Outing Magazine*, some with N.C. Wyeth illustrations). Gathered into novel form in 1907, the realistic adventures featured a cowboy with a limp. (That's right: a cowboy with a limp.) He was

Stunt man Yakima Canutt takes a fall over buried planks in *Army Girl* (1938).

William Boyd as Hopalong Cassidy in *Renegade Trail* (1939).

called "Hopalong," was red-headed, swore, drank and would be changed completely when film producer Harry Sherman put him in The Movies.[9]

"Pop" Sherman felt he could do with Mulford's stories what Fox and Paramount had done with the Zane Grey novels. Mulford agreed, Paramount said it would release the pictures — that was when Sherman's first choice to play Hoppy, James Gleason, raised his acting price and lost the job — and in 1934, Sherman selected a 1910 Bar 20 novel called *Hopalong Cassidy* to kick off the series. That was also when he decided to go with Boyd, his second choice to play Hoppy.

By the time the Cassidys had run their course in the theaters, the shrewd Boyd had bought up all the rights. He made those pictures available to that new-fangled thing called Television and people fell in love with Hoppy all

William Boyd led different trios through the years.

The most popular trio is at left: Andy Clyde as California Carlson, Boyd and Russell Hayden as Lucky Jenkins. Next: the first trio: Jimmy Ellison as Johnny Nelson, George (later Gabby) Hayes as Windy and Boyd. At the bottom: the last trio, Clyde, Boyd and Rand Brooks as Lucky.

Robert Mitchum (l) and TV's Superman, George Reeves, were in several Hoppys up at Lone Pine. This is *Bar 20*. (And of course, Mitchum *starred* in two Westerns here.)

over again. More importantly (in a general sense), they fell in love with Westerns again.

Thanks to Hoppy's success, the Alabama Hills were re-introduced to movie-watchers and to movie-*makers*. Cowboy heroes racing through the Alabams became standard TV fare during the '50s as studios followed Boyd's lead and not only dusted off their own old Westerns for television but were encouraged to continue making new ones for the theaters (like the still-good Tim Holt series from RKO.)

TV Westerns of the '50s headed up the trail to Lone Pine, too, shows like *The Lone Ranger*, *Wild Bill Hickok*, *Bonanza*, so many more.

They continued making movies and mak-

[4] All the men who rode in the early Westerns say they really did gallop across an area as a group of crooks, then quickly change hats or shirts or both and ride across the very same area, this time playing the posse chasing themselves. That isn't just one of those Hollywood stories you always hear. It really happened.

[5] "In 1937," Henry Olivas told the Chamber, "the unions came in and we had to decide whether we were wranglers or actors. My brother Pete decided he was an actor and joined the Screen Actors Guild. I decided to stick to wrangling and joined Teamsters Local 87 out of Bakersfield. Here in the Valley, we wound up with about 24 extras and around the same number of wranglers."

[6] A 1938 tank vs. cavalry film from Republic starring Preston Foster.

[7] The same bluffs used by Warner Brothers in 1952 for Gary Cooper's *Springfield Rifle*.

[8] Charles Starrett is second, having played the Durango Kid in 65 Columbia features.

[9] In that first *Hop-A-Long Cassidy* movie, Cassidy was shot in the leg and as he was recuperating, he made what those familiar with the Mulford stories thought was an acknowledgement of the source material when he limped out one day and said he could "hop along with the best of them." Actually, that came about accidentally. Sherman wasn't going to explain the nickname at all until Boyd fell off his horse and broke his leg. So Sherman wrote in the leg wound. (The re-release was called *Hopalong Cassidy Enters*.)

so many were here

Clockwise from right we see Randolph Scott, who made several Westerns in Lone Pine during the '50s, Roy Rogers and Ken Maynard giving a ride to the ladies (that's Sheila Ryan with Rogers; she would become Mrs. Pat Buttram), Clint Eastwood as *Joe Kidd* (with Paul Kosla), Hoot Gibson (center) in the silent *Ridin' Kid From Powder River* (1924) and below, stopping a wagon are the stars of one of the best (and still enjoyable) series of Westerns from the late '40s and '50's, Tim Holt, right, and Richard Martin (whose continuing character of Chito Jose Gonzales Bustamante Rafferty he actually originated in the two RKO Westerns Robert Mitchum made, *Nevada* and *West of the Pecos*.)

eight man-made reminders from the movie days can still be seen out there

Among the man-made movie left-overs still in the Alabama Hills are the rock arrastra from 1948's *Yellow Sky* (ore was ground in an arrastra) and the concrete waterhole from 1950's *Mule Train*. Here, from left, are Gregg Barton, Gene Autry and Boyd Stockman. An edge of the canvas-covered waterhole is in the lower right corner.

ing memories on location in Lone Pine. And you can still find exactly where they worked — not only by matching photos to the terrain but by finding the *physical* evidence of the movie-makers' presence.

There's still some left — the arrastra Gregory Peck and those guys hid in in *Yellow Sky*, the rock wall where Autry/Yrigoyen jumped the convertible on horseback (was that part of a ramp for the jump or a ranch gate wall in some other film?). Then there are the remnants of the concrete ramps and supports at the *Gunga Din* suspension bridge location, the heavy eye-hook bolts stuck right into the rocks to hold up the *Tycoon* mine facade at Ruiz Hill, similar bolts up at the Cooper Rock campsite location for who knows what, the remains of the old asphalt road to a *Gunga Din* location and the concrete waterholes from Gregory Peck's *The Gunfighter* and Autry's *Mule Train*.

How could such relics remain after so long?

"In this arid climate, earth scars heal slowly," said Genny Schumacher in *Deepest Valley*. "Hills ripped open by gold seekers," she went on, "(and) gullies torn by cloudbursts look as fresh and raw as they did a hundred years ago." Add movie-making to that. Certainly, all the roads are living testimony.

This whole area is virtually criss-crossed with the dirt roads and trails made 30, 40, 50 years ago by the movie companies to get their heavy and bulky equipment into the back country.

Today, those (lower case) movie roads make touring this movie country easy but don't, please, depend only on that car. It's not until you get *off* those roads that you really appreciate the Alabama Hills.

You have to be on foot — deep amid those towering boulders — to really feel the magic. That's where the fun is: ducking underneath low overhangs, following twisted paths through tight crevices, then suddenly coming upon a spot you recognize.

Look, John Wayne rode right by there in a wagon in *Blue Steel!* And Gabby was drivin'! And right over *there*...

next — we're going where these were shot

Gary Cooper leads a patrol (heading east toward Gary Cooper Rock) in *Lives of a Bengal Lancer* (1935), Gregory Peck and Anne Baxter near the 1948 *Yellow Sky* set (just off Movie Road) and Gene Autry's radio caravan rolls through Pot-sa-ga-wa Gardens in *Melody Ranch* (1940). That's Lone Pine Peak to the right. And on its left flank, you can see run-off gullies which take on a goblet shape, known locally as the "Wishbone."

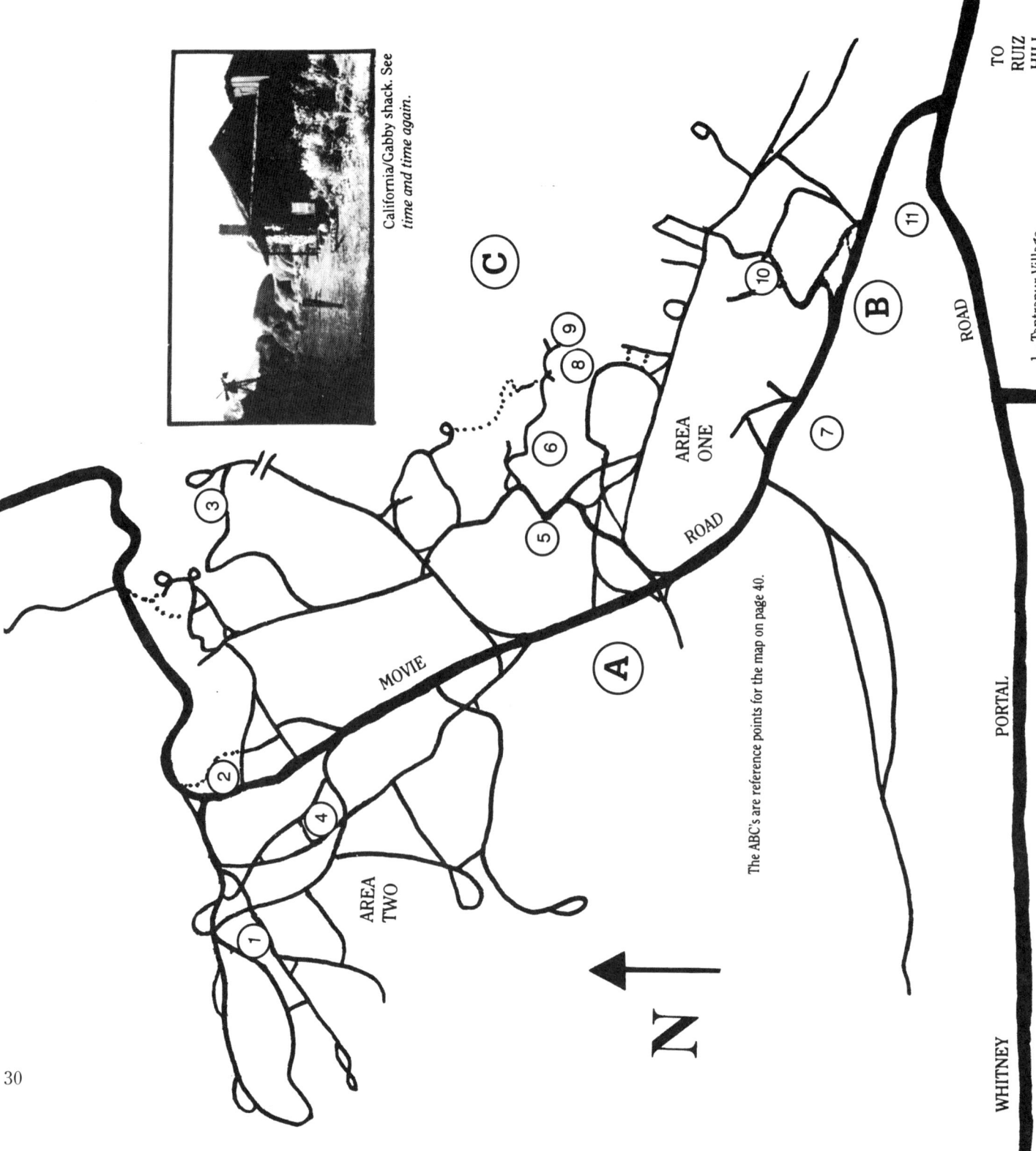

California/Gabby shack. See *time and time again.*

1 - Tantrapur Village.
2 - *Rawhide* stage station.
3 - California-Gabby house.
4 - *Rawhide* burial site.
5 - *Lone Ranger* ambush site.
6 - Gene Autry Rock.
7 - *Gunga Din* tent city.
8 - Bengal Curve.
9 - Gary Cooper Rock.
10 - *Yellow Sky* set.
11 - Red Dog town.
12 - where Johnny stopped the stage in *Bar 20 Rides Again.*
13 - *Gunga Din* temple pocket.
14 - A *Gunga Din* 'discharge papers' scene (see below).
15 - where Johnny was ambushed in *Bar 20 Rides Again.*
16 - where John Wayne and his Singing Riders captured Black Bart's gang in *Westward Ho.*

The ABC's are reference points for the map on page 40.

major filming areas we'll guide you to

Areas One and Two are detailed on subsequent pages. Many of the individual locations seen here will also be found on those more detailed maps and numbered again in relationship to those illustrations (i.e., the 1938 *Lone Ranger* ambush site is (5) here, (27) on the *area one detail* and (37) in the "Hoppy Rocks" photo.)

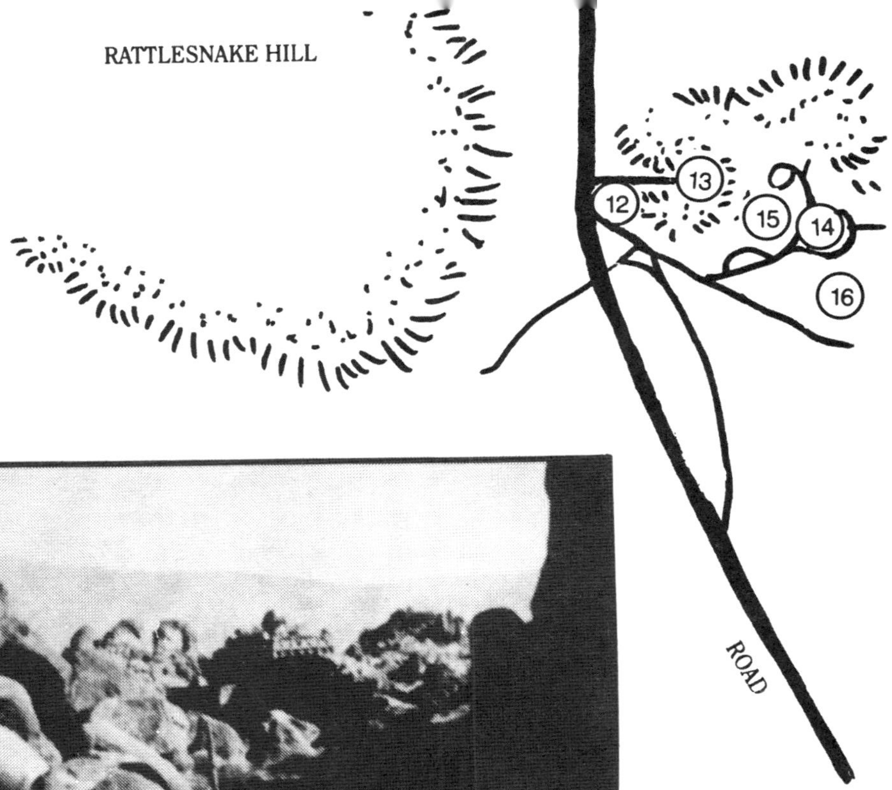

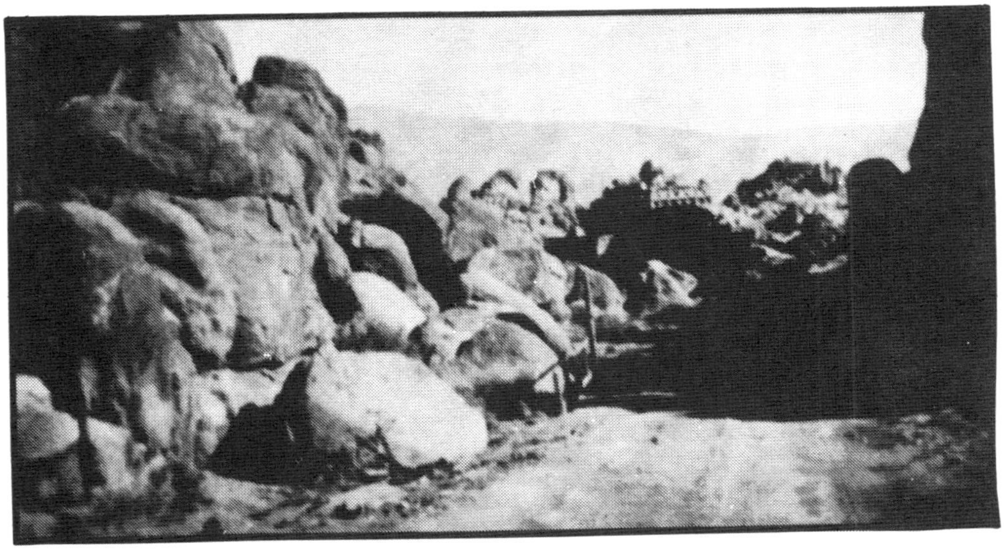

RATTLESNAKE HILL
12
13
14
15
16
ROAD

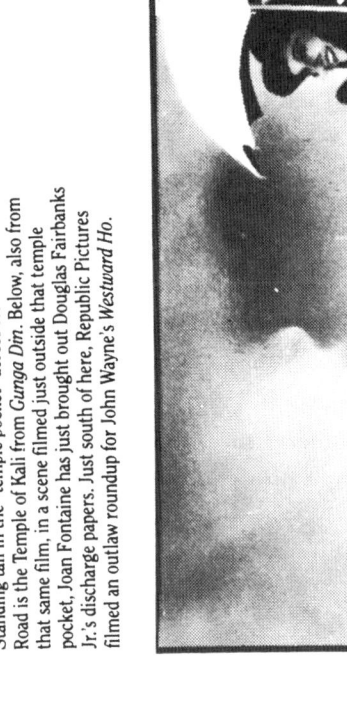

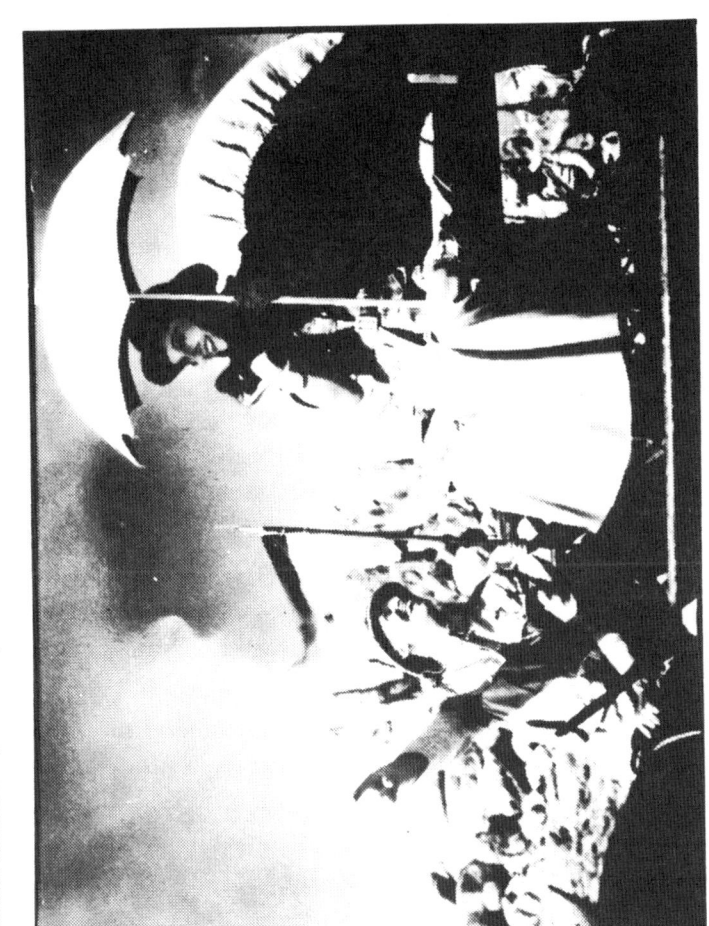

Standing tall in the "temple pocket" across Horseshow Meadow Road is the Temple of Kali from *Gunga Din*. Below, also from that same film, in a scene filmed just outside that temple pocket, Joan Fontaine has just brought out Douglas Fairbanks Jr.'s discharge papers. Just south of here, Republic Pictures filmed an outlaw roundup for John Wayne's *Westward Ho*.

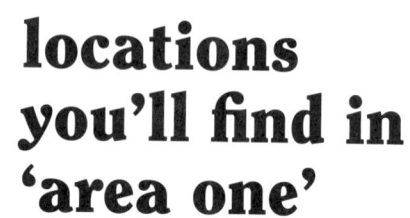

locations you'll find in 'area one'

Top left: It was the first time on screen for the "Lone Ranger ambush" – the cornerstone of the masked man's legend when outlaws killed every Texas Ranger in the group but one, leaving a lone survivor, a lone Ranger – and it was shot in Lone Pine for the 1938 Republic serial, *The Lone Ranger*. And you'll find *where* it was shot on the maps for *area one*, as you'll find the locations for (continuing clockwise) this stagecoach holdup just up Lone Ranger Canyon (from Randolph Scott's *Hangman's Knot* with Frank Faylen the cop in It's A Wonderful Life and Dobie's dad on TV's *Dobie Gillis*, on top and where Joe Yrigoyen doubled Gene Autry jumping Peggy Stewart's convertible in Trail To San Antone. Next: Errol Flynn in a scene from Kim (it was on this trip that Flynn signed the wall in Lone Pine's Indian Trading Post) and two shots on the Movie Road from *Charge of the Light Brigade*, the first featuring from left, David Niven, Patric Knowles and Flynn, the other showing the caravans parading by Light Brigade Rock.

up at the gary cooper rock

During a battle in 1935's *Lives of a Bengal Lancer*, an undercover agent leapt from the top of this protruding rock to run down the hill, pretend to be shot and fall near Gary Cooper and Franchot Tone to pass on some vital information (although they filmed *that* dialogue three-quarters of a mile from here; see the *area two* photos). That unique and very thick horizontal stone is Gary Cooper Rock (Cooper is seen at left in a scene *not* in the movie).

Below we see (1) Audie Murphy and Felicia Farr beside it as gunmen crowd in and (2) a today shot with the author. It was also from up beside the Rock that MGM shot Errol Flynn looking down on a Russian encampment in *Kim*.

Go part-way down the hill from Gary Cooper Rock, move west (across some camp locations from *King of the Khyber Rifles* and *Comanche Station* which you'll learn about when you turn the page) and you'll find the *Bengal Lancers* view at the right (looking down onto Bengal Curve). At that point, you're also near where they shot the *Bengal Lancers* shot back on page 29.

MUCH OF THE ACTION in *King of the Khyber Rifles* (1953) also took place up near the Gary Cooper Rock. At the far bottom left: Tyrone Power awaits possible death at the Khyber Stakes location and at top far left, he walks to his movie brother's camp earlier in the film. (To orient you, the Cooper Rock is directly behind the camera here, up the hill.) To the camera's left is the Triple Camp location: the brother's native camp in *Khyber Rifles*, the camp in which Errol Flynn shot those Russians in *Kim* and the Indian camp at the beginning of *Comanche Station*.

Next: two views of the secret huts high atop the cliffs in Fox's 1925 telling of Zane Grey's *Riders of the Purple Sage* with Tom Mix.

On this page is the Three Passes area right by the Lone Ranger ambush site (just out of view to the left of the young man in the photo below.) Here, he's looking up the narrow pass where that wagon exploded in 1934's *Blue Steel* (with George Hayes and John Wayne aboard) and where Ken Maynard's pal was killed in *Fiddlin' Buckaroo* (1932).

(X) marks the spot in both photos of the pass John Wayne rode down in *Westward Ho* (1935) when he was heading for that ambush at the end of the picture. It also was the same pass — in *Secrets of the Wasteland* (1941) — through which Hopalong Cassidy and the Chinese escaped. (Match the photo above to the film; Hoppy and friends dashed out of the left pass, the bad guys gave chase on foot down the one on the right.)

Dashing to safety in *Secrets of the Wasteland*.

more 'area one' locations to find

all on the 'yellow sky' location

39

area one

To help orient you, this perspective is from the circled C on the preceding map with the A's and B's corresponding.

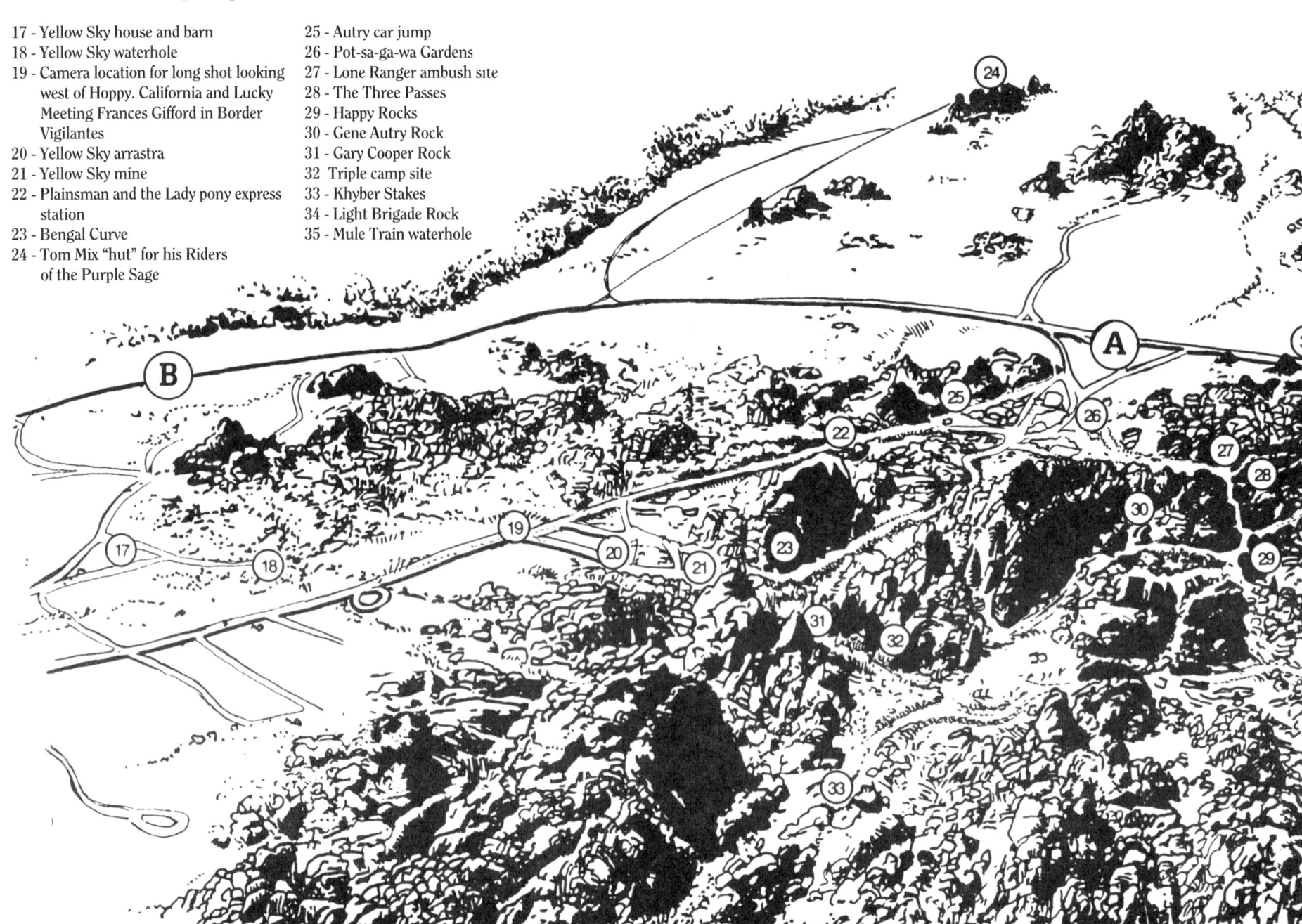

- 17 - Yellow Sky house and barn
- 18 - Yellow Sky waterhole
- 19 - Camera location for long shot looking west of Hoppy. California and Lucky Meeting Frances Gifford in Border Vigilantes
- 20 - Yellow Sky arrastra
- 21 - Yellow Sky mine
- 22 - Plainsman and the Lady pony express station
- 23 - Bengal Curve
- 24 - Tom Mix "hut" for his Riders of the Purple Sage
- 25 - Autry car jump
- 26 - Pot-sa-ga-wa Gardens
- 27 - Lone Ranger ambush site
- 28 - The Three Passes
- 29 - Happy Rocks
- 30 - Gene Autry Rock
- 31 - Gary Cooper Rock
- 32 - Triple camp site
- 33 - Khyber Stakes
- 34 - Light Brigade Rock
- 35 - Mule Train waterhole

AT THE 'HOPPY ROCKS' ...

36 Hopalong Cassidy and California Carlson (Wm. Boyd and Andy Clyde) hid from the men chasing them in *Silent Conflict*. Gene Autry and Pat Buttram hid there, too, in *Beyond the Purple Hills*. Just beyond these foreground rocks, Gene Autry came down the road from the right, following some suspicious wagon tracks in *Cow Town*.
37 The *Lone Ranger* ambush site.
38 The Three Passes.
39 Camera location for *Hangman's Knot* stagecoach shot.
40 Where they shot the stagecoach holdup in Tim Holt's *The Stagecoach Kid*.
41 Where Hoppy and the boys caught up with Quirt (Francis McDonald) in *Bar 20*.

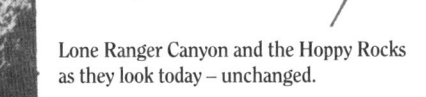

Lone Ranger Canyon and the Hoppy Rocks as they look today – unchanged.

Continuing on foot toward the Gene Autry Rock, you'll find...

42 - *Kim* camera location.
43 - Judge's camp in *The Devil's Playground*.
44 - where Hoppy found the body in *The Devil's Playground*.
45 - where Glenn Strange rode to set up ambush in *False Colors*.
46 - where Indian attack in *How The West Was Won* began.
47 - where *Bengal Lancers* troops rode by.
48 - Autry, Burnette and boy here in *Boots and Saddles*.
49 - where Roy Rogers, Big Boy Williams and Duncan Renaldo stopped while looking for wild horses in *Hands Across the Border*.
50 - where boy held gun on Three Mesquiteers in *Gunsmoke Ranch*.
51 - Tim Holt tried ditching posse here in *Guns of Hate*.
52 - Indian Chief Noah Beery Jr. and Iron Eyes Cody started a wagon chase here in *Indian Agent*.
53 - Hoppy, California and Jimmy pass here to save ambush victim in *False Colors*.
54 - Tim Holt chased Steve Brodie (escaping in wagon) by here in *Guns of Hate*.
55 - Tyrone Power tied to stake in *King of the Khyber Rifles*.
56 - Gary Cooper Rock to the right.

William Boyd (r) helps Tom Seidel fight off the ambushers near the Gene Autry Rock in *False Colors*.

TO HOPPY RO

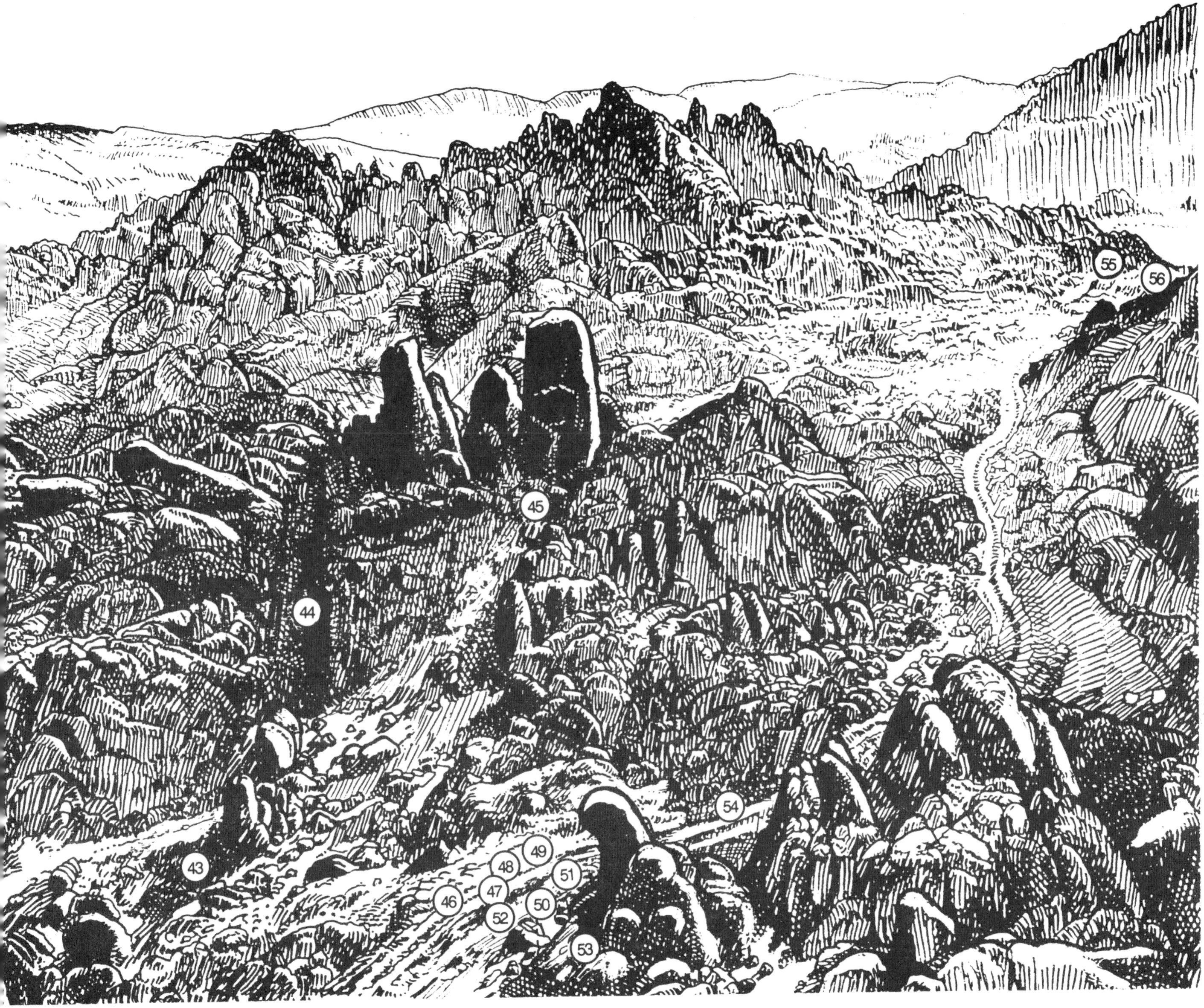
55
56
45
44
54
49
48
51
47
43
46
50
52
53

next comes 'area two'

where you'll find ...

that the 'gunga din' suspension bridge was barely off the ground

ALSO IN 'AREA TWO' was Tantrapur, the native village in *Gunga Din*. At the near left, Victor McLaglen tours the eight-acre village.

In *GUNGA DIN*, it looked like that suspension bridge – the one Cary Grant and Sam Jaffe are crossing at far top left – spanned a really deep chase . . . but no. In the "today" photo, you see hikers Bill Shelton and Michael Holland at each end of where the bridge was really strung (further verified by the 1938 snapshot taken from the village location by Ethel Olivas, who got to play on the bridge when no-one was looking).

you'll also find...

...SUCH LOCATIONS as (beginning at left) the canyon Fox used in the 1941 remake of *Riders of the Purple Sage* with George Montgomery (seen here), the "cattle pocket" where this rare photograph was taken for *Charge of the Light Brigade* ("rare" because this Surat Khan hunting party scene was not in the finished film) and an Errol Flynn portrait location for *Light Brigade*. This one's fun because it's a good "photo opportunity" spot for Lone Pine visitors today: easy to find and easy to match (as Holly Holland demonstrates at right). Take your picture where Errol Flynn did — with the Background Rocks behind you! They're called the Background Rocks because they're in the background of...

...MANY SCENES in many films, such as *Brigham Young* (left) with Tyrone Power and Linda Darnell (below left). And notice the rocks at the right side of this covered wagon shot. They're also in the photo below, taken five years earlier for *Lives of a Bengal Lancer*. This location was used to film the dialogue scene that audiences thought took place at the bottom of the hill at Area One's Gary Cooper Rock (that's the undercover agent just beyond the camera).

THE BACKGROUND ROCKS are not only easily spotted (left) behind the rooftop fighting in *Gunga Din* and (below left) in *How The West Was Won* — here, with frightened horses rushing by, Robert Preston picks up Debbie Reynolds (it's really stunt men Jack Williams and Loren Janes) — but in other films, as well, over the years. Hoppy, California and Lucky followed an outlaw by here in *In Old Colorado* and Hoppy's life was saved by none other than Robert Mitchum here in *Bar 20* (see the *area two* map). Below, they're (where else) in the background (so is the *Rawhide* burial site) as turbanned soldier-actors of *Lives of a Bengal Lancer* (1935) line up for lunch right where scenes for two Hopalong Cassidy pictures were filmed (*Three on the Trail* the next year and *Heart of Arizona*, 1938) and where Gene Autry made camp in *Comin' Round the Mountain* (1937).

Photo by Kerry Powell

As noted in the *Gunga Din* chapter, there were so many troops and Thuggees in that film's final battles, they matched the activity of a disturbed ant hill. This one was at No. 62 at right.

area two

57 The Background Rocks, so-called because they were in the background when, among other scenes in other films, the Sergeants Three were fighting on the rooftops of Tantrapur, the village built for *Gunga Din* at 58. See *time and time again* for more such scenes.

59 where Robert Mitchum saved Hopalong Cassidy's life in *Bar 20* (he pushed away Victor Jory's gun as Jory was about to shoot Cassidy, pretending to be a wounded outlaw in the back of a wagon).

60 where Robert Preston scooped up Debbie Reynolds as the wagons raced by in *How The West Was Won* (it was really stunt men Jack Williams and Loren Janes).

61 where Errol Flynn posed for that *Charge of the Light Brigade* portrait.

62 *Gunga Din* fight here.

63 This is the "cattle pocket." Pete Olivas said that when cattle were needed for an early morning shot, they would be driven over from the Anchor the night before ("driven" as in herded, not trucked) and kept in this protected pocket overnight.

64 The *Rawhide* burial site.

65 Site of the *Rawhide* stage station.

66 where Lucky was wounded in *Heart of Arizona*.

67 where the Hindu horsemen swept around the rocks in that village fight at the beginning of *Gunga Din*.

68 where (1) Hoppy stopped the stage in *Heart of Arizona,* where (2) Gene Autry camped when he broke that wild horse he'd saved from the wolves in *Comin' Round the Mountain* and (3) the crooks chased Hoot Gibson by here in *Lucky Terror*.

69 *Gunga Din* suspension bridge here.

70 overlook of George Montgomery in his *Riders of the Purple Sage*.

71 where Natalie Wood stopped Tony Curtis and Keenan Wynn in *The Great Race*.

93 The covered wagon overturns rolling into ravine with Debbie Reynolds (again Loren Janes) tumbling inside.

COUSIN FLAT

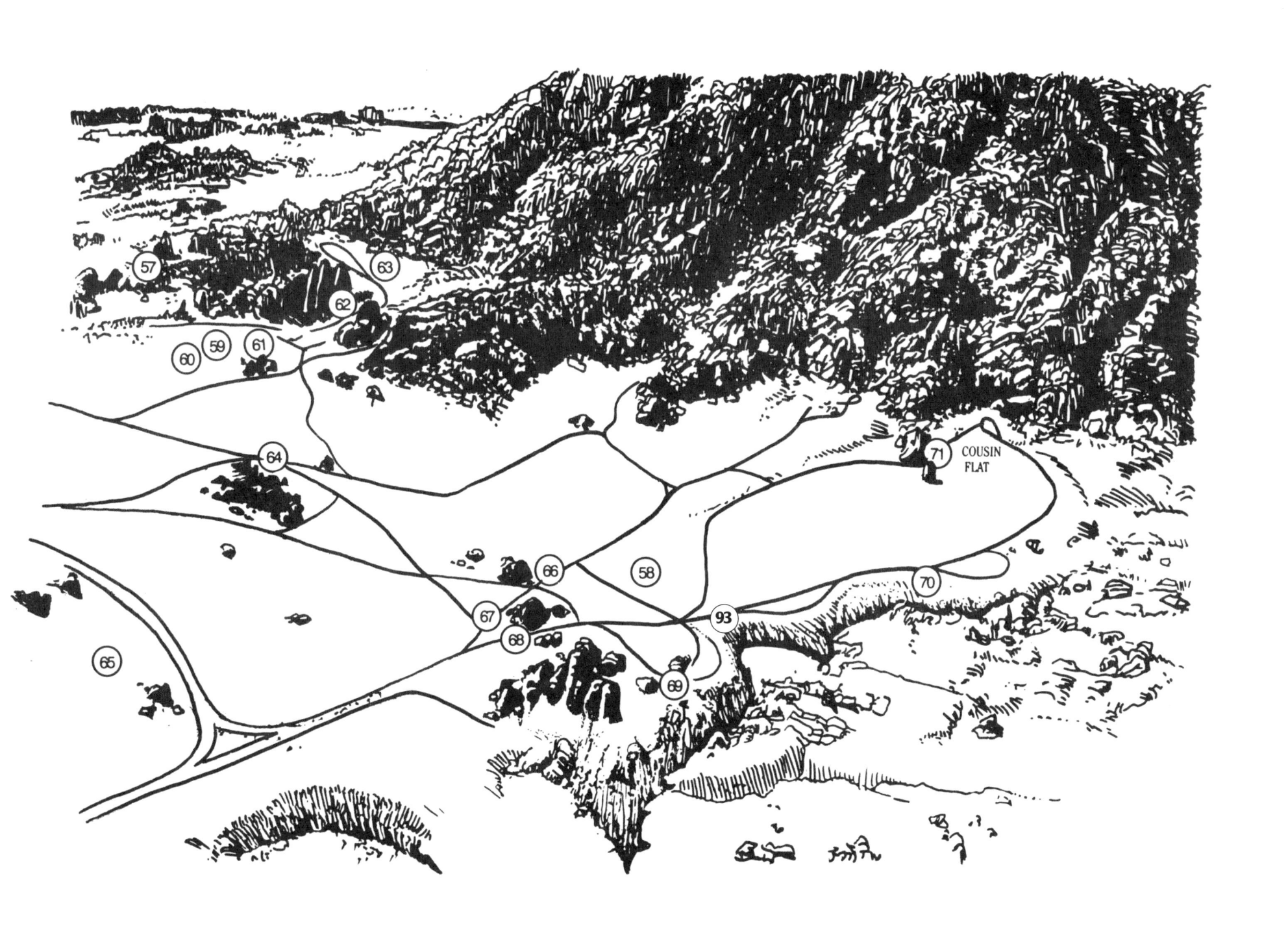

also in area two:

the stage station at Rawhide Pass

Tyrone Power was just learning the business when outlaws took over his stage station in Fox's *Rawhide* (1951) to hold up the in-coming coach. Below left, veteran villain Jack Elam keeps his good eye on Power. Below, Susan Hayward is in the coach as William Haade talks to the passengers. The two men at left are Edgar Buchanan and Max Terhune, the latter a long-time member of Republic's Three Mesquiteers.

The rock formations at the left are easy to spot from Movie Road when you're looking for where the *Rawhide* set was (that's the water trough out back of the station). But you'll notice the photo below was taken at almost the same spot and at almost the same time of day — but this one was taken *five years later* with Randolph Scott for his *Seven Men From Now*. Also at this same spot, George Hayes was shot and killed in the first Hopalong Cassidy film, made 15 years *prior* to *Rawhide*. (Gabby was called Uncle Ben in that one).

**next:
where they shot 'tycoon**

**gene and hoppy and
the lone ranger
were there, too**

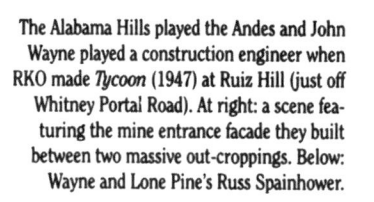

The Alabama Hills played the Andes and John Wayne played a construction engineer when RKO made *Tycoon* (1947) at Ruiz Hill (just off Whitney Portal Road). At right: a scene featuring the mine entrance facade they built between two massive out-croppings. Below: Wayne and Lone Pine's Russ Spainhower.

TOM MIX was here for a couple of scenes in *Riders of the Purple Sage*. And his location at right (we're looking south) was a pretty busy area (see the map).

The face of Skull Rock was where director Wm. Witney (top right with camera) shot stunt man Yakima Canutt doubling Lee Powell in the 1938 serial, *The Lone Ranger*.

Below, Lone Pine visitors assume similar poses at the grotesque landmark, unchanged for 52 years except for the graffiti.

all shot
at ruiz hill

ruiz hill was a major location for the 1939 classic, 'gunga din'

a fleet of busses and trucks brought the company here

57

ruiz hill

Located behind Skull Rock, Ruiz Hill was one of the more popular filming spots over the years. Pronouced ROO-ees (not Roo-EEZ) Hill, it took its name from an early ranching family, whose ranch house was in this pocket.

72 - The back of Skull Rock (aka Gorilla Rock). On the other side: the Canutt jump for *The Lone Ranger*, the 1938 serial.
73 - Wayne and Spainhower on *Tycoon* set.
74 - Cannon location in *Gunga Din*.
75 - Outlaws observed posse at 81 from here in *Rootin' Tootin' Rhythm*.
76 - Location of dugout in Autry's *Rootin' Tootin' Rhythm*.
77 - Where Johnny was captured near end of *Bar 20 Rides Again*.
78 - A *Gunga Din* battle.
79 - Mine facade in *Tycoon* stretched between 79 and 80.
81 - Other *Gunga Din* shots in this area (troops, elephants, etc. in the relief column).
82 - Up behind here: the Tom Mix camp in *Riders of the Purple Sage*.
83 - On other side of outcropping: where Mix examined the "Masked Rider" in *Riders of the Purple Sage*.
84 - Where Tony stood in that shot.
85 - In Autry's *Cow Town*, Ted Mapes (who doubled Gary Cooper a lot) and Chuck Roberson (who doubled John Wayne) hid here and were killed by Harry Shannon (who was such a nice old fella in *Song of Texas* (!)). Autry here, too, investigating.
86 - Victor Jory's gang had its hideout cabin here in *BorderVigilantes* (this was the time Hoppy threw a bandanna full of cartridges into the fire.)
87 - Where Hoppy and Windy (Gabby) hid in the long shot of that gun-fight at end of *Bar 20 Rides Again*.
88 - In *Kim*, Errol Flynn examined that campfire here.
89 - Another *Gunga Din* battle.
90 - Gunsight Pass where (1) the *Gunga Din* relief column came through (with Thuggees clinging to the rocks above, as seen from 91 and where (2) Hoppy was ambushed by Hal Taliaferro in *Border Vigilantes*. Also was (3) the entrance to Pico's outlaw hideout in *Three Men From Texas*. (It was here and in that film that California (Andy Clyde) told Hoppy that the lookout's warning horn was "the mating call of the bull camino.")
92 - Another *Gunga Din* battle.

on-site instructions —
keep turning to your right;
Gunsight Pass is behind you

Young Sammy McKim gets the drop on the Three Mesquiteers, from left, Max Terhune, Ray 'Crash' Corrigan and Bob Livingston (two years before he was the screen's second Lone Ranger.)

time and time again

If you've seen 'em once, you've seen 'em a hundred times... a modified old saying that holds true with quite a few of the rocks throughout the Alabama Hills. They do tend to pop up again and again in various movies.

And why not? If a particular spot looked good to one film-maker, it often looked just as good to others. That's why you see Gene Autry Rock so often.

Another popular location was Area One's Lone Ranger ambush site. That was also where (1) John Wayne escaped his own ambush in *Westward Ho* (1935), where California and Johnny trapped those horses at the beginning of *Outlaws of the Desert* (1941) (and where Hopalong Cassidy rode the wild Thundercloud) and where (3) Roy Rogers, Duncan Renaldo and Guinn 'Big Boy' Williams headed off another bunch of wild horses in 1943's *Hands Across The Border*, trying to lasso Trigger. (When you visit the area, you'll see why this spot was often used for horse work; it was easy to fence in and thus easy to control "free-running" horses here.)

Some other locations used repeatedly (and not covered elsewhere) were:

THE HOPPY CABIN - Private property on Tuttle Creek Road; no trespassing, please. This was used in at least six Hopalong Cassidy Westerns (see the caption on the next page), plus Bill Cody's *Frontier Days* (1935), Ken Maynard's *Western Frontier* (1935), *Gunsmoke Ranch* (1937) with the Three Mesquiteers, Tim Holt's *Stagecoach Kid* (1949) and *Mysterious Desperado* (1949), Gary Cooper's *Springfield Rifle* (1952), Glenn Ford's *The Violent Men* (1954) and Randolph Scott's *Seven Men From Now* (1956).

LIGHT BRIGADE ROCK - In addition to scenes done in the area for Errol Flynn's *Charge of the Light Brigade* (1936), you'll also recognize the slope of the rock in Gene Autry's *Cow Town* (1950). This was where Jock Mahoney was escaping in a wagon -- until Autry used a lasso trick to yank the rear wheels off.

RAWHIDE BURIAL SITE - Also shot here were the scenes where (1) Robert Preston yanked Gregory Peck out of that wagon in *How The West Was Won* (1962), where (2) Hopalong Cassidy captured Sidney Blackmer in *Law of the Pampas* (1939) and it was by here that (3) outlaws chased the Three Mesquiteers in *Gunsmoke Ranch* (1937). You'll also see those distinctive rock columns way in the background when Smiley Burnette and the boys are trailing Autry and later when Gene is breaking that wild horse in *Comin' Round the Mountain* (1937) and when he's singing the title tune at the end of *Boots and Saddles* (1937).

POT-SA-GA-WA GARDENS - So-called from the days when Paiute Indians from the local

A POPULAR SPOT - Gene Autry Rock was in 1937's *Boots and Saddles* (a repeat photo at far top left) and in 1935, troops rode by it in *Lives of a Bengal Lancer*. Also here in 1937: Republic's popular cowboy trio, the Three Mesquiteers (match the rocks behind the boy). And in the 'today' shot, a visitor studies the spot in *The Devil's Playground* (1946) where Hopalong Cassidy found Shorty's body (an easy spot to find because, as here, you can see Gene Autry Rock in the background in that scene in the film.) Above, it even pops up in this shot commemorating a live piano concert Lone Pine once held in the Alabama Hills.

Reservation put on ceremonial dances here, different portions of this area is always popping up in films.

Hoppy and California drove cattle across here in *Silent Conflict* (1947), Robert Mitchum and Richard Martin galloped toward the sound of gunfire across here in *West of the Pecos* (1945) and you've already seen a photo of Gene Autry's radio show caravan driving across here in *Melody Ranch* (1940).

And where Autry (Yrigoyen) jumped that horse over the convertible in *Trail To San Antone* (1946) is the exact spot where (11 years earlier) John Wayne strung a rope across the trail and tripped the four horses and riders chasing him in *Westward Ho*.

This was a favorite Autry road. He galloped along here (chasing Little Spud) in *Boots and Saddles* and after leaving the pony express station in *Comin' Round the Mountain*.

William Elliott and Joseph Schildkraut had their final shoot-out in *Plainsman and the Lady* (1946) in the Gardens and outlaws had a corral here in *Heart of Arizona* (1938) (just south of the Lone Ranger ambush site).

And in an all-star scene for *Trail To San Antone*, Autry rode a horse he'd lassoed up to Peggy Stewart, whereupon Bill Henry socked Tris Coffin (with Sterling Holloway looking on), all in the one scene. Right here in Pot-sa-ga-wa Gardens.

THE HOPPY CABIN on Tuttle Creek Road was used in so many films, among them at least six Hoppys. Here, villain Harry Worth, left, talks to Lois Wilde and William Boyd (Hopalong Cassidy) at the cabin's so-easy-to-recognize well in *Hopalong Rides Again* (1937). Other Hoppys included *Bar 20 Rides Again* (1935), *Pride of the West* (1938), *Heart Of Arizona* (1938), *Renegade Trail* (1939) and *Colt Comrades* (1943).

'RAWHIDE' BURIAL SITE. Here, Tyrone Power and Susan Hayward buried Edgar Buchanan in *Rawhide* (1951) with Jack Elam (on horseback) and Dean Jagger looking on. See text for some of the other scenes where this unique formation can be seen.

ONLY RARELY did a movie set remain standing for any length of time out in the rocks. One that did was this old shack, seen time and again but seen first in the 1941 Hoppy, *Pirates On Horseback*. In that one, it belonged to California's cousin and in *Bar 20* (1943), it was the hideout cabin of Victor Jory's gang (this was the one Robert Mitchum was bringing the ransom to) *and* it was a ranch house belonging to Gabby Hayes in *Utah* (1945) — remember Grant Withers trying to talk Dale Evans into selling out as they stood right by that front porch? The lady on the porch here is Joy Anderson's older sister, Jeanne Spainhower, who wrote on the back of this snapshot: "I tell people this is my house — then I show 'em the other one!"

Joan Fontaine, Douglas Fairbanks Jr., Cary Grant and Victor McLaglen in *Gunga Din*.

**next:
when RKO made
the big one**

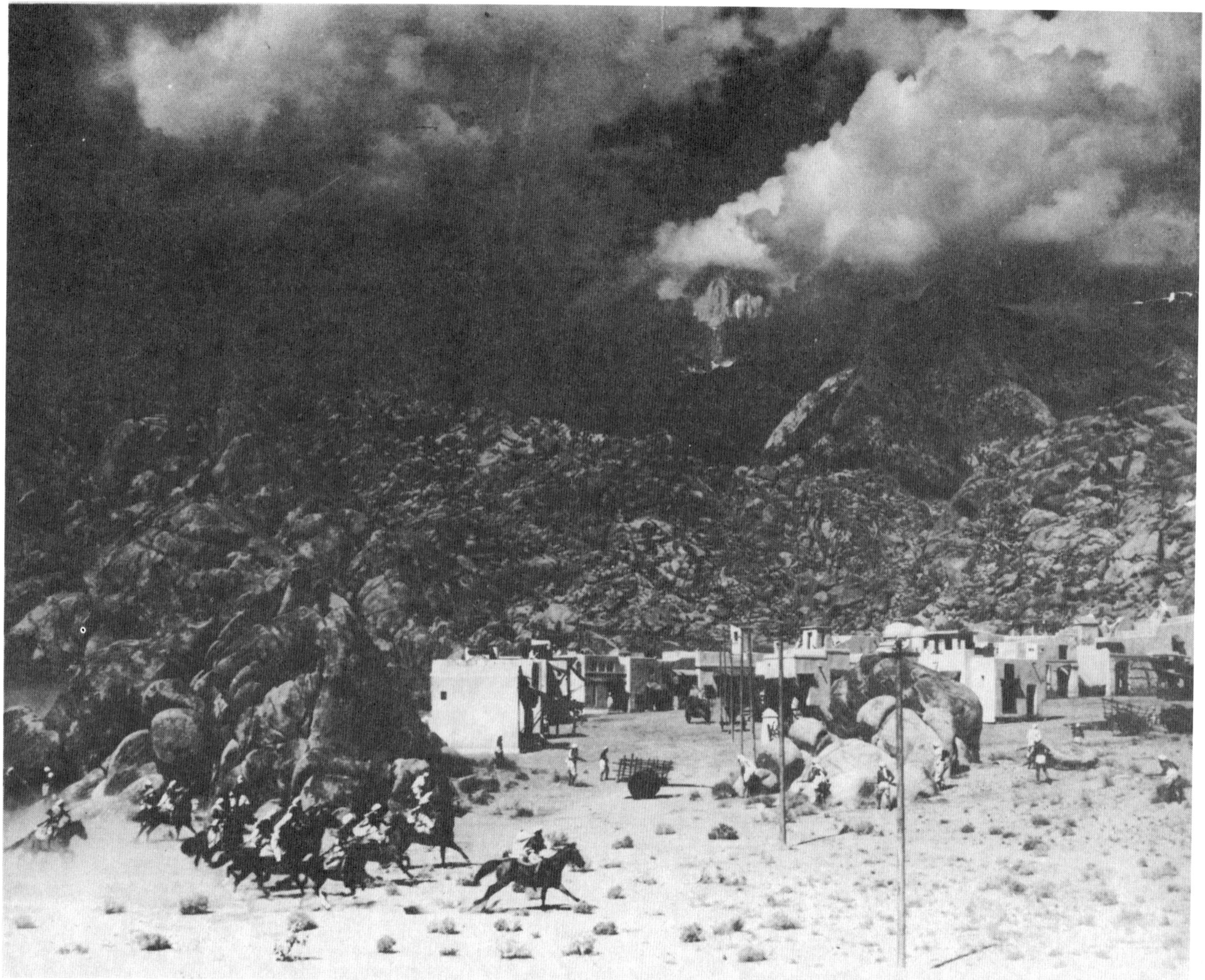

gunga din
the making of a classic

Cary Grant, Victor McLaglen and Douglas Fairbanks Jr.

It's Lone Pine's hallmark film.

It was the biggest, most ambitious production RKO had done up to that time (shot in 1938, released in 1939) and certainly the biggest ever done in Lone Pine. One still gasps in awe and wonder at "all those *people*, all those *horses*!" in the sweeping panoramas of its spectacular final battle. "My God, look, there's even *elephants*!"

It isn't often that "breath-taking" applies accurately to movie scenes but it does at the end of *Gunga Din*. Disturb an ant-hill and watch all those hundreds of little guys scurrying every which-a-way and that's the end of *Gunga Din*. (And please pronounce it 'Deeen,' as they do in the film.)

It was indeed a mammoth undertaking.

They spent a total of 10 weeks on location in Lone Pine (eight the summer of 1938, living in a tent city, then back for an additional two weeks that October). These were preceded by several weeks of construction on the gold-domed Hindu Temple of Kali (in that pocket in the rocks just off Horseshoe Meadow Road by Rattlesnake Hill), the huge fort and parade ground (along what is now Indian Springs Drive south of Tuttle Creek) and the nearly eight-acre native village of Tantrapur at the north end of Movie Flats to the left of the 'T' — *plus* a massive tent city just off Movie Road at the south end for the cast and crew!

There were more than a thousand extras in the big battle scenes — one report says 1,200, director George Stevens himself said it was 1,500 — bringing about a persistent Hollywood/*Gunga Din* story.

When discussing Lone Pine movies, a question that often pops up is, "Is it true they had to borrow bed sheets from the people in Lone Pine to finish costuming all those extras in *Gunga Din*?"

Well, it's almost true.

It has long been bandied about that there were so many native bad guys fighting the British on screen that RKO ran out of those wrap-around white costumes and had to quickly borrow bed sheets in town to make do, often paying to yank them right off clotheslines in their haste. Unfortunately (because it's such a great story), no-one I spoke to in Lone Pine remembered anything about that. Fortunately, another man did.

When writer George E. Turner was researching his 1982 *American Cinematographer* article on the picture,[1] he came upon the truth in the extensive RKO archives.

It seems some of the "Hindus" did need new costumes overnight (the fabric wasn't photographing right) so the wardrobe people did have to dash into town — but not to scavenge, darn it; to buy up all the flat white goods available (300 yards from the town's three stores). And yes, some 70 bed sheets *were* pressed into service but these were confiscated from tents in the location camp, not from town, alas. Thus the bed sheet mystery put to bed.

It took four weeks for a crew of 200 to set up that tent city, the living quarters and galleys, at which time (July of 1938) an unusually large company came up from Los Angeles: 16 cars, 12 trucks, 10 30-passenger busses, plus a large portable film laboratory.

During the shoot, the temperatures ranged from 105 to 115 degrees beneath "cloudless, empty skies," Director of Photography Joseph August recalled, then there would be "the most beautiful cloud formations I've ever seen," he said, as wind storms, dust storms and rain storms hit the location.

The sets had been built more solidly than usual — considerable stunt action would take place on the rooftops of both the temple and the native village — and no sooner had they finished the village and dressed it than a fire broke out, destroying a full block. The carpenters were brought back up from Hollywood and rebuilt it in 10 days.

As you can tell, they had just tons of fun.

All this madness began with Rudyard Kipling's 1892 poem, "Gunga Din," a stirring tribute to India's native regimental water carriers who, 'though often abused, trudged dutifully along with the British troops in their endless campaigns along that country's mountainous northwest boundaries.

In it, a private is so moved by one water boy's heroism and self-sacrifice in helping the wounded that the soldier cries out, "You're a better man than I am, Gunga Din!"

It wasn't in "Gunga Din" but in a previously published collection of short stories called "Soldiers Three" that Kipling wrote of the humorous adventures of three British privates in India. MGM gets the credit for first combining these two basic themes when they were considering the project in 1928. Five writers off-and-on worked on treatments there, all of which were shelved when Irving Thalberg dropped the project in 1931.

Independent producer Edward Small[2] bought the rights to the title from Kipling's widow in 1936 — he had optioned the poem once before — had work done on it, then lost control when he joined RKO as a producer. As part of that arrangement, the studio took over all of Small's literary properties.

That fall, producer-director Howard Hawks also joined the studio, still flush with his success on such films as *The Crowd Roars*, *Scarface*, *Twentieth Century*, *Barbary Coast*, *Ceiling Zero* and *The Road To Glory*.[3] He was quickly assigned *Gunga Din*.

By this time, nine writers had worked on the script over the years but Hawks started fresh with long-time friends and collaborators Ben Hecht and Charles MacArthur.

Hecht and MacArthur, of course, will always be remembered for that classic (and hilarious) play, *The Front Page*. In that Broadway triumph, you remember, ace reporter Hildy Johnson is leaving the newspaper to get married, chucking it all, much to the shock and dismay of his colleagues who conspire to get him back. In *Gunga Din*, Sergeant Ballantine is leaving the Army to get married, chucking it all, much to the shock and dismay of his colleagues who conspire to get him back. And around that familiar and successful hook, Hawks, Hecht and MacArthur fleshed out the characters and came up with many of the elements we know from the film today: adding the elephant medicine to the punch at the ball, the

Sam Jaffe as *Gunga Din*.

---

[1] As noted in *acknowledgements*, the other prime source for *Gunga Din* details was Rudy Behlmer's excellent "AMERICA'S FAVORITE MOVIES/Behind the Scenes," a book published in 1982 by Frederick Ungar Publishing, New York. In it, he indeed goes behind the scenes to tell how 15 classic movies were made (*Casablanca*, *The Adventures of Robin Hood*, *Stagecoach*, etc.). In his introduction, he says "the purpose behind this work is to reveal the creative process of the collaborative system of film making." He does that with wit and style and masses of information.

Other footnotes at end of chapter.

The large British cantonment RKO put up on what is now Indian Springs Road was one of three massive sets built on location in Lone Pine.

elephant pushing down the jail wall to rescue Cutter, Cutter's capture at the temple, etc.

During this period, they also began discussing casting.

Hawks wanted to borrow Robert Montgomery and Spencer Tracy from MGM to play Ballantine and MacChesney. RKO production head Sam Briskin instead asked Metro for Clark Gable, Tracy and Franchot Tone.[4]

MGM did loan RKO the Marx Brothers — no, not for this, for *Room Service* — but wouldn't deal over Gable, Tracy and Tone so by mid-1937, *Gunga Din* was back on the shelf and Small, Hawks and Briskin had all left RKO. Happily, RKO's new production chief, Pandro S. Berman, also saw the potential of the project and put still another writer on it. But even so, he later admitted being "awfully worried about cost."[5]

Should he bring Hawks back to direct? Hawks, who seemed so reckless with time and money? "Howard was rather slow and difficult," Berman once recalled, "and I was afraid he would go over budget so much that I would be in trouble...so I went with George Stevens who, up to that time, had made pictures quite reasonably for us[6]...but lo and behold, when Stevens got on *Din*, he became as slow as Hawks ever was and perhaps a little slower!"

Even after they got on location, the script was still being worked on; any production will slow to a crawl when you don't know who says what or does what. And once in Lone Pine, Stevens reverted to the silent film techniques he had learned as a Hal Roach cameraman on Westerns and Laurel and Hardy comedies: figure out after dinner what you would do the next day. You have to shoot *some*-thing while the typewriters are clacking away into the night.

But whatever his pace, it sure seems justified today in retrospect because Stevens was assembling a winner. He had felt that from the start.

He said he always knew exactly where he wanted to shoot it: "In California around Lone Pine...a rather remarkable area because there are the Sierras at their best, Whitney and the other peaks...and those Alabama Hills, this strange rugged rock formation..." It is said that Stevens "knew the place well," having previously shot some Westerns there and certainly, he had seen how effective the area was as India in *The Lives Of A Bengal Lancer* (1935) and *The Charge of the Light Brigade* (1936).

"We designed the sets before the script was (finished)," he later recalled. He and art director Perry Ferguson flew up to Lone Pine "and laid out the three sets: the temple, the town and the parade ground."

Next, with production scheduled to start within weeks, Stevens hurried off to Arrowhead with the last pair of writers, Joel Sayre and Fred Guiol.

The Hawks-Hecht-MacArthur collaboration had developed the characters and worked out action and bits a'plenty but it lacked cohesion, Stevens felt, the one "thing necesary to glue (it all) together." Guiol's research turned up that missing element.

In the virtual library on India he had taken along to the mountain lake resort, he found an article about a secret society of native Thuggee killers devoted to the goddess Kali, who supposedly demanded human sacrifice. The Thuggees were a real-life cult who terrorized India between the thirteenth and nineteenth centuries, killing more than a million people. They all carried strangling cloths since they were forbidden to spill blood but even more chilling was the fact that they also carried small pickaxes so they could dig the

At Left, entering Tantrapur to investigate the broken message. At right, the final scene, filmed down at the Olancha sand dunes. The actor playing Rudyard Kipling was Reginald Sheffield, real-life father of Johnny Sheffield, Tarzan's "Boy."

graves of their victims ahead of time.

They were getting something on paper; now they needed a cast.

Individually, we remember the Soldiers Three this way:

An older Cary Grant comes to mind first: that daring but debonair fellow in *To Catch A Thief* or *Charade* or when he's being chased by that bi-plane in *North By Northwest*. Or at his fast-talking younger best in *His Girl Friday*.

Victor McLaglen? You can't forget him stammering his way to an Oscar in *The Informer*, as the blustery Sergeant-Major in *She Wore A Yellow Ribbon* or taking on John Wayne in *The Quiet Man* (all for John Ford).

And when it came to dash and style, The Movies had no-one quite the match of Douglas Fairbanks, Jr., not even his *Robin Hood* of a father in my opinion — particularly in such swashbuckling favorites as *Sinbad The Sailor* and that true masterpiece of the genre, *The Exile* (both of which also spotlighted the acrobatics of stunt man David Sharpe.) But collectively, we'll always see those three in Kipling khaki. They will forever be what Stevens called the "Rover Boys in India" — Sergeants Cutter, MacChesney and Ballantine off on another adventure, accompanied by Sam Jaffe as Gunga Din, the water boy whose fondest wish was to be a soldier, the same Sam Jaffe who had played the High Lama in *Lost Horizon* the year before and would later be the senior Doctor on TV's *Ben Casey*.[7]

McLaglen was borrowed from Fox to play MacChesney and Joan Fontaine, then a young RKO contract player, was set to play the love interest.[8]

Jack Oakie, also under contract to RKO, was discussed at this point to play Cutter with Cary Grant, with whom the studio had a non-exclusive agreement, as Ballantine. But that changed when Doug Jr. got involved.

Fairbanks recently told an interviewer on cable TV's superb "American Movie Classics" that he and Grant were good friends even then and one day, Grant told him "there was a discussion of doing a film around the British Army in India and it would be great fun if you and I could do this together.'

"I said that sounded grand but 'which part did you have in mind for me to play?'

"'Decide yourself,'" he said Grant told him, whereupon Fairbanks suggested they toss a coin. They did and that's how, according to Fairbanks, he became Ballantine and Grant became Cutter, names they continued to use between themselves for years.

"I'd get a telephone call," Fairbanks smiled, "and the operator would say, 'It's a Sergeant Cutter' and I knew it was Cary calling to say hello.'"

So, like Flynn and Cooper and Tone and Niven and Patric Knowles before them, Grant, McLaglen and Doug Jr. were fighting for the Empire and in so doing, riding across Movie Flats into cinematic history. They almost didn't finish that ride, however; not in Lone Pine, anyway.

They were running considerably over budget and over schedule what with re-writing and improvising and the unpredictable weather delaying them ever further. Set to shoot six weeks in Lone Pine, they shot seven, then eight and they still weren't finished with the outdoor scenes. Finished or not, Berman and the New York office were growing more and more alarmed at the escalating costs.

"They wanted to cancel the film," Fairbanks remembered, "but we ignored the

Continued on page 72

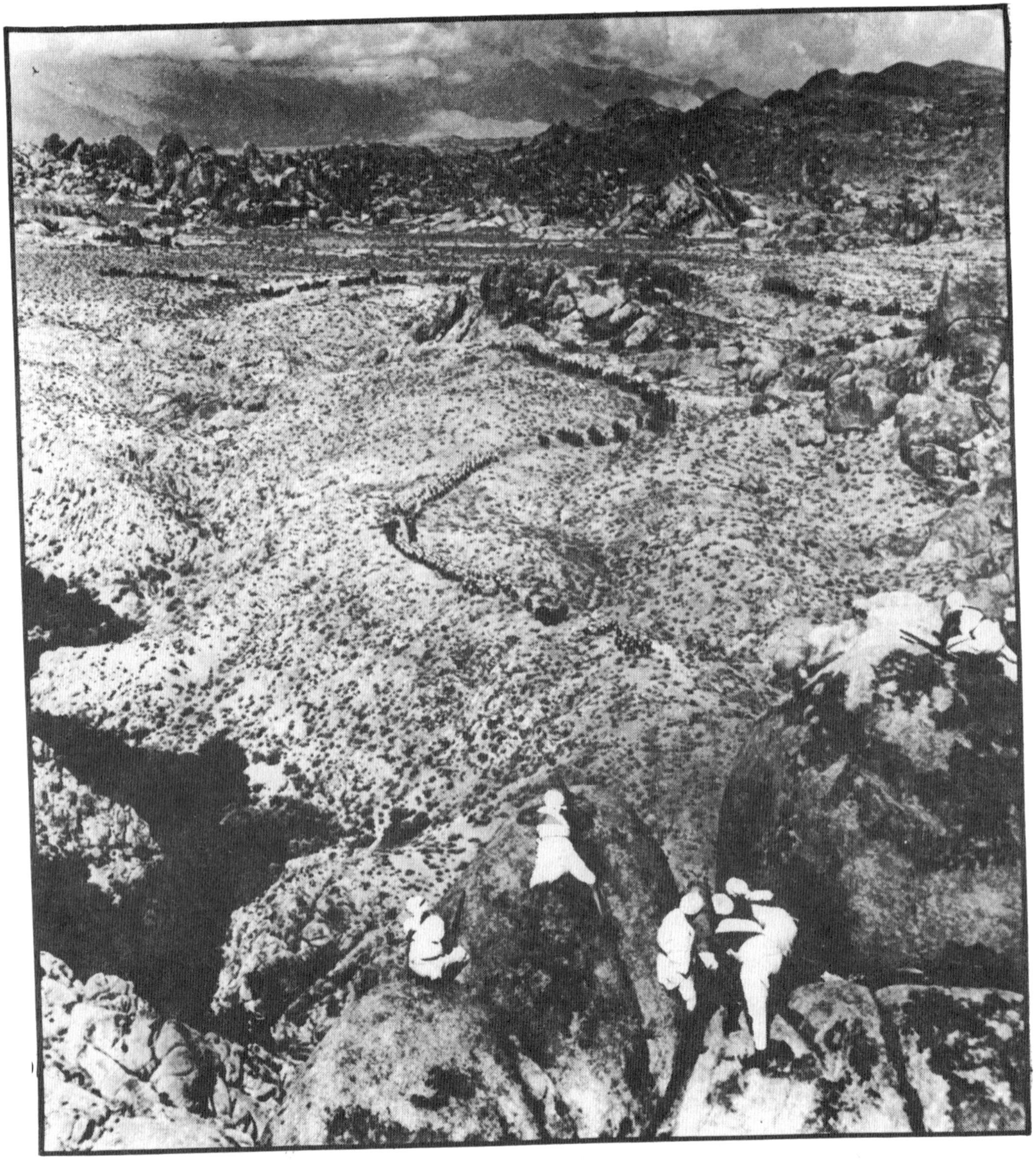

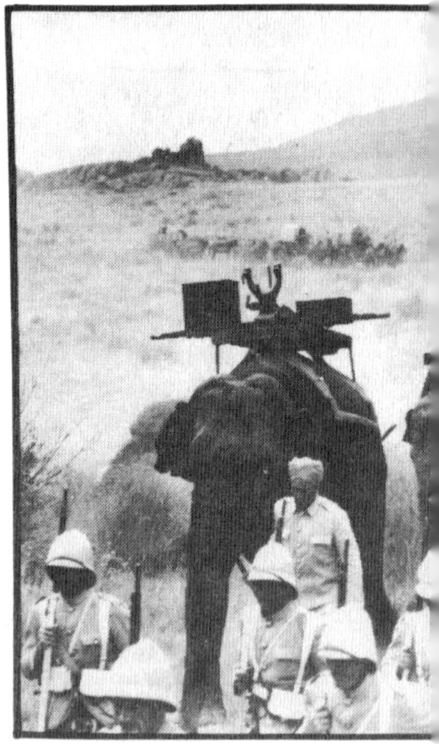

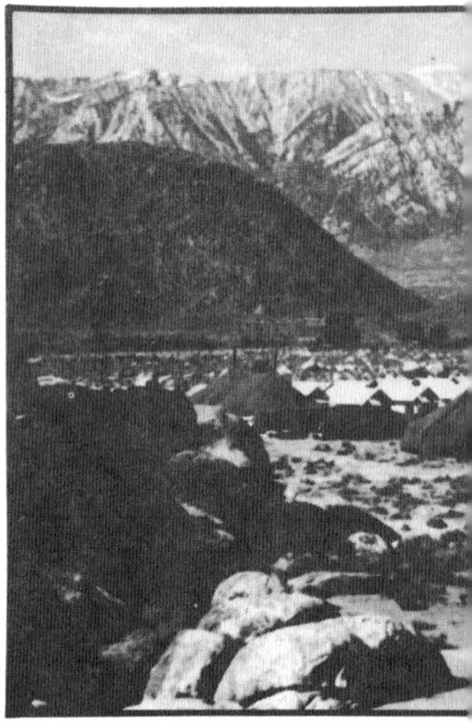

between the extras and the elephants, it really was a big 'location' picture

Director George Stevens said there were 1,500 extras on location in Lone Pine for the final battle scenes and it did look it. Here we see the huge relief column winding its way across the rocky terrain to rescue the Sergeants Three. The shot at far left was taken a few 100 yards east of the power poles near the end of Shahar Road (you do not have to cross private property to find it) and in the shot at top middle, the column is approaching the east end of Indian Springs Road. The fort, where we see them filming above, was on Indian Springs. And the tent city at left, where everyone lived, was on Movie Road. More than 300 people lived in these tents for most of the shoot. That included nearly 40 in the commissary staff alone (cooks, bakers, dish-washers, etc.) The size of the entire location party more than tripled in October of 1938 when the company returned for the final battles with all those extras. (One more note: Fifteen thousand pounds of ice were brought up from Los Angeles each week to keep eack week's 14 tons of meat and vegetables refrigerated.

Continued from page 69

messages for several days and kept on shooting, knowing there wasn't much they could do about it because we were right in the middle of the desert, way, way out at a place called Lone Pine or beyond…"

Finally, the company was ordered home.

While the Lone Pine footage was reviewed and cut into sequence, many of the remaining scenes were shot at locations nearer the studio; they built a village street up in Bronson Canyon in Hollywood, Lake Sherwood (out near Westlake) doubled for the lake at the edge of the village and interiors and temple-top scenes were shot on the Hollywood lot and on the RKO-Pathe lot in Culver City.

And then the studio executives saw a rough cut of what they had so far. No music,[9] no effects, just fantastic footage and the more they saw of it, the more they loved it — so much so that an extremely courageous decision was made.

Despite the fact that the final cost of the film would almost certainly exceed what could be brought in at the boxoffice in first run release,[10] it was decided — based on the quality of the material shot thus far — to authorize an even bigger ending than they had planned originally. They wanted to make this "a truly spectacular production, to go all-out and stage a magnificent battle finale."[11]

So the company was sent back up to Lone Pine for an additional two weeks work. Naturally, they got there just in time for a pre-season snowstorm.

The rugged mountains had been established in the background with no snow, then overnight, they *had* snow and Stevens and August had to shoot close-ups or at least angles that avoided the mountains until the Sierras melted "back to normal."

But fighting Mother Nature was child's play compared to the real job before them.

"The job," George Stevens himself said, "was to use 1,500 men, several hundred horses and mules — to say nothing of four elephants — most effectively for scenes of utmost confusion…

"To do this, we first fought the entire battle on paper (including) the charge and the headlong retreat of the Thugs. Then we transferred our activities to Mount Whitney's slopes and rehearsed the cast in small detachments and in slow motion until the mechanics of the action were established.

"As the scene took shape, the number of people and animals was gradually increased (and) the action speeded up until we had the scene going at top speed. Then we shot it."

For the sake of simplicity, he made it sound like it was done on one grand field, all at once, but it was much, *much* more complicated than that, quite a logistical triumph.

At the end of the story, you remember, the three sergeants and Gunga Din are all on top of the temple, prisoners of the fanatical Guru (Eduardo Cianelli) as a mammoth relief column of soldiers marches to their rescue. Hundreds of the Thuggee killers wait in ambush — "the best mountain fighters in the world," the Guru says — clinging to rocks overlooking the pass, hiding in crevices, crouched behind boulders, their strangle-cloths at the ready.

Lining up a shot of the Temple of Kali in the Temple Pocket off Horseshoe Meadow Road.

It was filmed and edited to appear that the column came slowly across the flat, through the single pass (off Horseshoe Meadow Road) where it was ruthlessly attacked, hundreds of horsemen dashing down first this canyon, then that, cannon firing across this valley, Thuggees chased up that slope – all right around the temple. But no.

Actually – movie-makers are usually quite practical, after all – most of the battle scenes and the approach shots were staged in less confining expanses miles away from the temple location. (And don't forget that since the column was saved from certain annihilation by Gunga Din climbing tortuously to the top of the temple's gold dome with that bugle and blowing a warning call, only to die a hero's death, that these "most important" scenes were shot down in Hollywood, some 200 miles away).

Drive out into the Alabama Hills and match photos in this book to the terrain and you can find where they filmed many of the battle scenes.

The *medium* shots of the approaching column – rescuers getting closer and closer, men lined up four abreast with elephants and bagpipers and supply wagons strung out forever behind them – were shot some three miles away from the temple, across from the fort set off what is now Indian Springs road (with close-ups of the soldiers and the officers done four miles from *there* on Movie Road).

Those stunning long shots of the troop winding across that great expanse – one cut opens with a close-up of a Thug with binoculars, then slowly pans across the hiding Hindus to look down on the approaching and very distant column – were shot from that cluster of high rocks east of what is now the end of Shahar Lane. From the dirt road that follows along the line of power poles, you can still see the eroded and scattered remnants of an asphalt road they made to get to that camera location.

The Thuggee horsemen and the infantry, all lined up and ready to *go were* shot from the top of the temple or appropriate platforms in the temple pocket east of Rattlesnake Hill, as were some of those late afternoon (back-lit) concluding skirmishes.

There was also a fight at the suspension bridge location and some of the massive troop movements and Thuggee chases were done out on Movie Flats and in and around the "cattle pocket."

"Just beyond the range of the cameras," Stevens said, "were posted first-aid facilities as well as wranglers to re-capture frightened riderless horses. Behind various rocks, assistant directors kept in touch with me by field telephone and relayed my "commands" to the groups nearest them."

Other battle scenes were done at Ruiz Hill: Gunsight Pass doubled for the narrow entrance to the temple pocket in a couple of shots and after "masters" were gotten – long shots of whole areas – the cameras were moved onto that center rise of the Ruiz pocket and the action was staged on three sides of them. They could shoot to the front, then turn and shoot to the side, then turn and shoot behind them. That, too, sounds more simple than it was. Each "turn and shoot" took hours to set up.

But they got it done. It worked.

It worked so well that when most people watch *Gunga Din* today, they don't see the hard work represented, just the results of that work, which is the way it's supposed to be.

Let them think that the battle was all done in one day at one spot, that one day they wrote a script, then got on the bus and went out and shot it in the Valle somewhere. (Weren't all movies done that way?) That won't stop you taking this book with its maps and photos out into the rocks at Lone Pine and saying, "Here's where they built the suspension bridge and look, right across the road is where the village was! Remember them throwing those sticks of dynamite to each other? That was right out *there*!

George Stevens (center) works with McLaglen and Doug Jr.

Others will just enjoy a good movie but you'll know.

[2] Over the years, his films included *Last of the Mohicans, Kit Carson, The Son of Monte Cristo, Up In Mabel's Room, Brewster's Millions* and *Davy Crockett, Indian Scout.*

[3] He would later direct such classics as *Bringing Up Baby, His Girl Friday, Sergeant York, To Have and Have Not, The Big Sleep* and *Red River.*

[4] Others considered along the way for the leads were Ronald Colman, Robert Donat, Roger Livesey and Madeleine Carroll.

[5] As well he should in those movie-going days of the '30s when tickets were a quarter or fifty cents and they had to give away dishes to coax people into the theaters. *Gunga Din's* final negative cost ended up at nearly two million dollars, an almost un-heard of figure for the period; only a few films (like *Hell's Angels* and *Gone With The Wind*) cost anywhere near that then.

[6] He had made *Alice Adams* with Katharine Hepburn and Fred MacMurray, *Annie Oakley* with Barbara Stanwyck and Preston Foster, *Swing Time* with Fred Astaire and Ginger Rogers, *Quality Street* with Hepburn and Franchot Tone, *A Damsel In Distress* with Astaire and Burns and Allen and most recently, *Vivacious Lady* with Ginger Rogers and Jimmy Stewart. (He would later do *Shane, Giant, Diary of Anne Frank* and *The Greatest Story Ever Told,* among others.)

[7] RKO had originally wanted Sabu to play the title role but Alexander Korda wouldn't release him. After the Indian boy's success in *Elephant Boy* and *Drums,* Korda was preparing *The Thief of Bagdad* for him.

[8] She had worked for Stevens in two pictures before, *Quality Street* and *A Damsel In Distress*. The later star of Hitchcock's *Rebecca* recently told an "American Movie Classics" interviewer that when she first got billing in a film, she and her mother took the then-terribly long drive over to Pasadena to enjoy it on the marquee and saw: JOAN FOUNTAIN. At least, it was close.

[9] Alfred Newman eventually did the exciting music for the picture. Erich Wolfgang Korngold (he scored *The Adventures of Robin Hood* among others) turned down the assignment when Berman couldn't give him the six weeks time he wanted to write the music. Newman did it in three weeks. (Remember Newman's equally stirring score for *Captain From Castile?* One of that piece's themes became the USC Trojan signature music.)

[10] Fortunately, the picture proved good enough to be re-issued periodically so it eventually did make money for the studio.

[11] Behlmer.

they remember when...

"If you're doin' a book on The Movies up here," I was told, "then you've got to talk to Pete Olivas. He started as a kid workin' in the movies, him and his brother both, and I'm talkin' about the *silent* pictures!"

And Rellis Amick and Della Cederburg, they said. They were waitresses here and can tell you lots of stories. And Della's sister, Ada Brown. She and her husband George had a ranch down at Olancha and "kept the stock in their barns for the companies shootin' out on the sand dunes there."

"We kept seven camels there for a week once," Mrs. Brown laughed. "And the Lone Ranger's horse, 'Hi Yo Silver.' I remember they braided his mane and tail every night, then combed it out the next morning."

And talk to Burl McElroy, they said. "He lived here during the '30s and '40s and has just returned after 30 years in the military. He used to work on some of the movies, just like his daddy before him."

"That's right," Burl McElroy told me. "I worked on *Yellow Sky* and *Bad Day At Black Rock* and *Tycoon*. Built roads and blasted holes and worked on the sets. My dad helped build the town of Red Dog and a whole lot more. See, the movie companies would just take the construction people off the county payroll and put 'em on the studio payroll. That's the kind of cooperation they got up here. Everyone knew how important The Movies were to the area."

Robbye Carrasco remembers catering lunches out in the rocks. "I was working for Johnny Morris at the Mount Whitney Cafe," she said. "All of us worked for Johnny at one time or another, I guess. He ran the Sierra before that." Remembered as "a great guy and an even better cook — oh, could that man cook," Johnny Morris catered lunches for The Movies. Other chefs people remember in town were Carl Countz and Bruce Morgan.[1]

"And lemme tell you somethin' about Roy and Gene and Hoppy," Robbye said. "They always told Johnny Morris that no matter how many kids were out on the set (town kids come out to watch the filming), to always feed 'em. Don't you ever turn those kids away at lunchtime, they told him."

Ethel Olivas (Pete's sister-in-law, Leakey's widow) remembers taking lunches out to the sets, too. But she remembers doing it in an earlier time, when she and her sister-in-law had to hitch up a chuck wagon and team to do it. She's 81 now. The Movies were around a long time.

And things were casual then.

Many people remember stars such as Randolph Scott coming into a restaurant at night for dinner, tired and still in costume. And they could do it without being mobbed. Lone Pine respected its visitors. These people were coming up here to work and work hard, an ethic Lone Pine could easily identify with. Lone Pine worked for a living, too. And Hollywood *was* paying its way, after all. But more to the point, the natives *liked* their paying guests.

In the end, they found the actors and producers and technicians to be "just folks, if allowed to be. So they didn't fawn over them. They let them walk the streets without being annoyed or harassed. They accepted them as people and the stars felt "at home" in Lone Pine. They could be themselves.

Once, Rellis Amick stopped to pet the big St. Bernard named "Bing" that belonged to Clarence Fashball, who ran the feed store here. Coming

Pete Olivas, right, and his brother Henry, left, in the early Movie Days with an unidentified friend.

---

[1] During the '50s, Morgan also managed the Dow and as such would help coordinate things for the movie people (Russ Spainhower was tapering off from those duties). Dorothy Bonnefin, who runs Lone Pine Realty now, worked for Morgan at the Dow then, helped him make movie arrangements and was even a dress extra once (at the officers' ball in *King of the Khyber Rifles*.)

around the corner were Rudy Henderson (who ran the lumber yard) and a visitor.

Not seeing the dog, they just overheard Rellis say, "Hiya, Bing! How are you?" "Just fine, thanks," the visitor said with a smile. "How are *you*?" It was Bing Crosby.

Ethel Olivas and her small daughter were visiting a Western set in the Alabamas and little Margaret said, "See that man on the horse there, Mama? That's the kind of saddle and bridle I want. Take a picture so we won't forget." So Ethel took a snap-shot of Gene Autry and Champion.

"The only time," Mrs. Amick said, "that I ever saw people go crazy over some stars was when June Allyson and Dick Powell stopped off at the Mt. Whitney Cafe for some tuna sandwiches. On their way back from Mammoth, I think. Well, people were all over them. We had to lock the windows!"

Rellis' sister-in-law has another memory of the Mt. Whitney.

"I remember," Robbye Carrasco said, "that Roy Rogers used to bring his guitar in almost every night and sing for everyone." "And that was after workin' all day out in the rocks," put in her husband, Harold "Swede" Carrasco. "He just loved to sing!"

I had run into the Carrascos out at Ruiz Hill as I was finishing up some mapping and photography of that busy Movies area. He's 67 and she's 64 and they had trailered their horses out to ride for an hour or so.

"I worked for the movies some myself," Swede volunteered. "I did some wranglin', I was an extra, I was even a stand-in for Gabby Hayes so he could rest while they were settin' th' lights and all."

"I remember," Pete Olivas said, "when Lone Pine Creek ran right through town. We used to fish right off the bridge, right in town."

He and I were driving through the Alabama Hills and he was pointing out some places and

When they shot out on the sand dunes at Olancha (at top: *Bagdad*, 1941), George and Ada Brown often kept the movie animals in their barn. Left, Burl McElroy's dad posed for the family Kodak on the *Tarzan's Desert Mystery* set (with Cheetah at the controls.)

sharing reminiscences. "This is where they rolled down the boulders on Tyrone Power and his men in *Khyber Rifles*... I worked on *Mule Train*, too, did I tell you that? Broke all them mules. They were all *pack* mules and we had to break 'em to harness... On *Rawhide*, they had two twin girls playin' the baby. One would cry, the other one wouldn't say much...It was either Buck Jones or Tom Mix, I'm not sure, used to bring his own cook crew up here and eat outside.[2] There were some really big barbecues..."

And one of Pete's stories reinforces the value of Russ Spainhower to The Movies.

Today, you can drive Movie Road from Whitney Portal Road all the way up across the old Moffatt Ranch to re-join 395 above the Alabama Gates five miles north of town. But when Fox made *Brigham Young* here, the road didn't go beyond the "T" at the north end of Movie Flats. And since they were also shooting up on the Moffatt, to get there, they had to go all the way back to town and take the highway around.

"So Russ got the county to cut the road through," Pete told me, "so companies could just cut across and not lose all that time going around. And look," he pointed. "See how the road hugs the hills (to the east)? He had 'em do it over there to keep the center area road-free for filming the big shots."

Not only did Lone Pine treat its visitors with respect but Hollywood wouldn't brook any nonsense or misbehavior on the part of its people, either. The bosses felt that being in Lone Pine was like being a guest in someone's home so they should conduct themselves accordingly. "Are they all behaving?" was a question asked often and with genuine concern of inn-keepers and waitresses in particular.

Actress Joan Bennett — so lovely in such diverse films as *The Macomber Affair* and *Father of the Bride* — was up here once, not as a performer but helping her husband, producer Walter Wanger, with production chores on *The Adventures of Hajii Baba*.

One of the film's young actresses was "acting up one night at dinner," it was remembered, and Joan Bennett got up from her table, walked over and whispered, "Knock it off or we'll send you home." "You can't do that!" the young woman protested. "I've got a big part!" "We'll write you out!" Joan Bennett promised.

That sort of story is common. Ace stunt woman Polly Burson had to straighten out one of her gals once: "Careful, honey! I can always get another rider!"

Often, the locals settled matters themselves. When Big Boy Williams threw a steak at waitress LaVerne Whiting, she threw it back at him! "Another time, the Dow Hotel management threw him out and he had to sleep on the bus," someone remembered.

But the bosses had the last word.

Rellis Amick remembers one abusive actor who was part of a group that came in late for dinner — they had shot late — and she had to ask them "to look at the menu and order before 10 o'clock, please; the chef's got someone sick in his family and has to leave early."

Everyone happily complied, "all but this one smart-aleck," she said.

"He waited 'til the deadline — past 10 o'clock when everyone else was already eating — then he orders steak and potatoes and a special this and that, stuff I just couldn't get him. Plus he kept makin' snippy remarks the whole time, 'No-one's gonna tell *me* when I can order!' Well,

---

[2] Both might have but Mix certainly did. In November of 1924, during a violent flare-up of the Los Angeles Owens Valley water dispute, when Valley men took over the Alabama Gates and diverted river water out of the aqueduct for five days, Mix was filming in the Alabama Hills – it must have been Riders of the Purple Sage – and took his orchestra and cook crew over there, providing a barbecue party for the assembled crowd.

Dedicated June 17, 2000, look for the commemorative plaque on the west side of Hwy. 395 and Mt. View St. Next to this plaque is the wood building (formerly La Florista Flower Shop) built by the Meysans in 1873. In the alley behind the structure is all that remains of the pre-earthquake Lone Pine. That protected adobe wall was part of the rear wall of the old general store.

The 1872 Earthquake

No-one had ever even imagined that one of the peaks in the Sierras was a volcano – not until the rumbling and shaking began at 2:30 on Tuesday morning in 1872. Then people saw the white-hot showers of sparks that flew from the crashing boulders tumbling down the mountains and thought surely, a volcano was erupting.

But it was "just" an earthquake, a tragic, devastating earthquake. The ground around the epicenter near Lone Pine dropped 10 to 20 feet vertically – look toward the Alabama Hills on both side of town; you can still see the western scarp line of the fault – and moved 12 to 16 feet horizontally. The broken fence lines were testimony to that.

Twenty four people died in Lone Pine that March 26th when some 60 of the small town town's 8- mud and adobe buildings crumbled and collapsed; a mass grave is just north of town

The shocks were felt as far north as Bishop; people in Camp Independence said the 'quake' lasted three minutes. Dust hung over the Sierras for two days.

Diaz Lake, thought by many of today's visitors to be man-made, was formed by "the great earthquake." Underground springs opened and the water flooded the low land where the earth had dropped that 20 feet. The lake was named after a prominent Lone Pine family of the time. (Don Raphael Diaz, a native of Chile, is buried in Lone Pine's pioneer cemetery.)

"It was not unusual to see cameras set up right in town" is always brought up in stories about The Movies in Lone Pine (as the photo of the unidentified company at left emphasizes). At top is Lloyds Western Wear (known to the locals as "the shoe shop"), located in the old bank building and thus the scene of many a movie holdup in the early days. Above are Swede and Robbye Carrasco on horseback at Ruiz Hill where they shared stories of the Movie Days.

none of us realized that three of the big bosses were in the next booth and the next day, they had him on the bus home!

That was in the Sierra Cafe (aka Sierra Trails). "It was a garage originally", Rellis Arnick remembered, "then a kindergarten. I even took tap dance lessons there once. It had quite a history even before it became the best place to eat in town."

There's a car wash there now; it's the one directly across from The Grill and diagonally across from the Dow Villa Motel. The town has changed some over the years.

Rudy Henderson's lumber yard was where the Whitney Portal Hostel, Merry Go Round and Seasons Restaurants are now. And the Catholic Church used to be where the Dow Villa Motel is now. Lynne Bunn of the Dow says "I used to go to bazaars in the basement of the church; that's where our swimming pool is." (She and her sister, Jeanne Willey, run the Dow Villa; they're the daughters of one of the two men who bought the Dow from the original owner, Walter Dow. He built it to accommodate the movie people.)

Where the pharmacy is (Lone Pine Drug Store), some remember Johnny Morris having a restaurant on that corner, too, for a while called "The Chinaman."

Bonanza Family Restaurant (great Mexican food) has metal decor depicting life in the Eastern Sierra and a local artist painting behind; look for the local flora and fauna. Many remember when it was a rooming house at one time and a dress shop and a drug store.

The Spanish Garden restaurant – there were great dances there and great steaks, they say – was next door to today's Thrift Shop. Just a vacant lot there, too, now. Yes, the town has changed some. But not the people.

Walk the streets and you still feel like you're a guest in someone's home.

Courtesy Eastern California Museum, Allan W. Ramsay collection.

Above and the close-up to the left is Lone Pines's Dow Hotel in the early days, flanked by the Lumber Yard and the Catholic Church. It was built in 1923 by G. Walter Dow to accommodate the large movie companies coming up regularly even then. (In 1925, he opened the Winnedumah Hotel in Independence). In 1957, the Dow's name was changed to the Dow Villa and the first motel units were added. Many remember the wood facade that was up for decades. How does the 2013 remodel compare to the original?

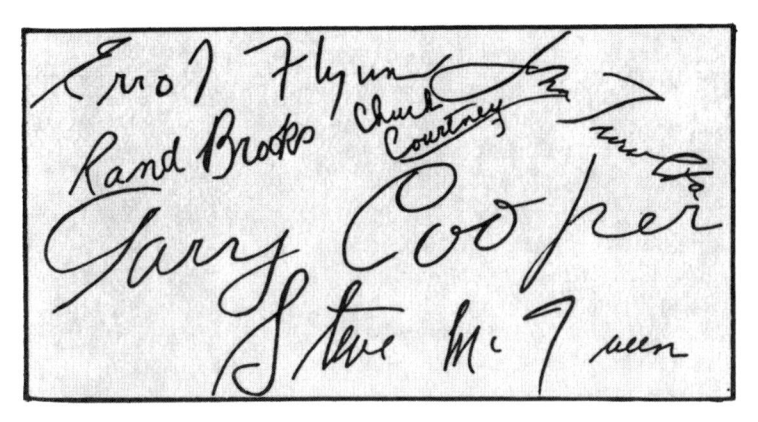

The Hand-Writing on the Wall – Literally

You can't help but remember the Movie Days when you walk inside Lone Pine's Indian Trading Post (at the traffic light corner, yes, there is still only one). That's where you'll find the signatures of many of the actors, actresses, directors, etc., who have been on location in Lone Pine – right on the store's walls and door frames. The movie people would stop in to shop, sign the wall in pen or pencil when requested, the signatures were burned in later.

You'll find so many there: Gary Cooper across the top of the front door, Gene Autry behind some Western belts, Jack Palance, Barbara Stanwyck, Edward G. Robinson, Tim Holt, so many, many more. Clayton Moore (TV's first Lone Ranger) signed in as Clay Moore; John Hart and Jay Silverheels are there, too.

And one of the favorite shop stories tells of Tyrone Power being behind the counter for some reason and waiting on some customers without being recognized!

Courtesy of the Eastern California Museum, Allan W. Ramsay Collection.

At first, the Lone Pine Hotel accomodated the movie visitors. You'll find shops and the Chamber of Commerce there now.

Cattle being driven down the middle of Main Street was not uncommon once, whether they were headed for some movie work or off to market.

the stories behind the names —
why do they call 'em the 'alabama' hills?

The exciting Westerns filmed in the Alabama Hills told of cattle drives, Indian battles and hold-ups, all of which really happened in and around Lone Pine in the 1800's. Art really has imitated Life here.

There was even a fight with the Paiutes out in the Alabama Hills once — shades of *How The West Was Won* — and the army from Camp Independence went out after bandits one lime—just like in *Yellow Sky*!

And another time — just like in *Rawhide* Tiburcio Vasquez and his bandits took over a stage station where he waited to rob the in-coming coach.

These things really happened so it seems appropriate — and it'll be fun — for us to look at the history of this land were visiting. But let's do it a little differently. Let's tell the story of the area by telling the stories behind its names.

It's easy to understand where names like "Movie Road" and "Gene Autry Rock" came from but what about "Lone Pine" itself and "Independence" and Bishop"? And why do they call 'em the *Alabama* Hills? And why is Mount Whitney called Mount Whitney? For that matter, which one is Mt. Whitney?? Let's settle that one first, even before we get to the history.

When first-timers to Lone Pine are having a meal at The Grill or Seasons, they can't help looking out the big windows at those gorgeous high Sierras — sometimes snow-capped, sometimes shrouded in heavy clouds, always awesome — and asking, "Which one is Mount Whitney?' So here are four facts that you can pass on to the next flat-lander *you* hear ask that.

First of all, the tallest mountain in the contiguous United States is not the tallest mountain you see from Lone Pine, That's Lone Pine Peak. It's the closest so it looks the tallest but it's really "only" 12,111 feet tall, The one we want is 14,495 feet tall and it's farther back and off to the right there, the one with the two jagged peaks just to its left. Look for this and you've found Mt. Whitney,

Second and this will really make 'em believe you were born here — the actual summit of Whitney's very sharp-looking peak is almost flat. Not only flat but large enough for a football field. Such are the tricks our eyes play from some 15 miles away.

Third, Mt. Whitney came within a signature of being called "Fishermen's Peak." Up until 1864, Northern California's Mount Shasta was considered the highest mountain in the West but then, a State Geological Survey party discovered that several peaks in the Sierra were higher. The tallest was named after the party's chief, Josiah D. Whitney.

Later on, there was confusion as to which peak was really Mt. Whitney When that was settled in 1873, three fishermen[1] climbed the true Whitney and christened it — what else? — "Fishermen's Pealk." - Some of the locals said they liked that name better than "Mount Whitney" — they didn't like Josiah Whitney; they didn't think he had investigated their big earthquake thoroughly enough — so they had their legislator introduce a bill re-naming the peak. But the governor refused to sign it and Mount Whitney it is. The First paths to its summit, by the way, were scratched out in the 1880's by astronomers, far cries from the graded walkway of today.

"And did you know," you can say as you get to the fourth fact that will astonish the flat-landers, "that this is the land of 20-mile shadows?" Don't be worried saying that; it's true. Mt. Whitney and friends cast shadows that are 20 miles long.

Some sundown when you're in town (clouds permitting), look east toward the Inyo Mountains and you'll see that while their tops still have sun, the entire Valley is in evening shade. And the Valley's 20 miles wide here. (And the name "Inyo"? It's the Paiute Indian word for "dwelling place of a great spirit")

The Mount Whitney group of mountains, incidentally, is much more formidable than you might imagine. It isn't just a bunch of peaks with one taller than the rest.

This particular grouping is actually a massive *granite wall* more than two miles high and 15 miles long (!) stretching from Mt. Langley

---

[1] Charles Begole, A.H. Johnson and John Lucas

**The movie wagon trains
were echoes of a real frontier past**

north to Mt. Tyndall. And between Olancha and Big Pine, there are 11 other peaks besides Whitney which are taller than 14,000 feet![2]

the alabama hills

When you head west toward the mountains from Lone Pine and enter the canyon with those tall hills looming up on either side of you —one is marked with the big white letters 'LP' —you have already entered the Alabama Hills. The name does not just apply to the rock protrusions in the valley beyond. And it was in these rounded hills during the Civil War —1863 to be exact — that Southern sympathizers discovered placer gold.[3]

At the time, a real go-get-'em Confederate cruiser, the *Alabama*, was in the process of sinking more than six million dollars worth of Northern shipping, so to celebrate her recent victories, the Johnny Rebs named their mines after her. Soon, the name applied to the entire range.[4]

And speaking of the "LP" on that second hill, Hazel Shultz told me she remembers the youngsters in town being paid to go cover those letters when they were filming on this side of the hills, "then they'd go put 'em back when the movie people left."

The hill just before the "LP" one (the first one you pass, the one right by the "Alabama Hills" name monument) is called Hoodlums' Peak, Pete Olivas told me, because of the hoboes who camped there during the Depression. At its base, where there used to be a hobo jungle, you can still see remnants from an even earlier time, the exploratory beginnings of a mine shaft and the rock walls of dugouts from the mining days. And from the Movie Days, Olivas remembers seeing cowboy film star Ken Maynard ride a horse down its steep slopes, "dust and rocks just a' flyin'."

As you enter the canyon, that small tunnel into the hill on the south side of the road is where the town's hardware stores stored their dynamite long ago.

lone pine

As for "Lone Pine" itself, that name came from a mining party camped along the creek in 1860 (possibly the Dr. Darwin French party from Visalia which came through here that year on its way to look for Death Valley's legendary Lost Gunsight Mine. They didn't find that — no-one has yet — but did discover silver in the Cosa range southeast of Olancha; maps still show a townsite of Darwin.)

Whoever the miners were,[5] they named the site "Lone Pine" after a tall Jeffrey pine standing where they pitched camp — Browning says it was where Lone Pine Creek and Tuttle Creek[6] converged (if they did once join, it was obviously before the Los Angeles Aqueduct truncated them) — a lone Jeffrey pine long since washed away by flood,[7] the history books say.

why the 'owens' valley?

Obviously, many place names hereabouts came from the names of pioneers and explorers who came to the Valley more than 100 years ago. It was only natural that the men making those first maps (and faced with dozens of nameless rivers and mountains and valleys) named many of them after themselves or people in their own expeditions.

Certainly that was true for the Owens Valley itself (and the same-named river and lake). Here's that story:

It was the search for beaver, gold and silver — any of which could earn men fortunes — that brought about the discovery and settlement of the Valley.

Mountain Man Joseph Walker was the first white man to enter the Owens Valley.[8] In 1833, trappers in Salt Lake City wanted to invade the massive Sierras but the vast desert was a flat but awesome barrier.

Walker was an experienced trapper and trail blazer so was hired to go exploring, to find routes from Salt Lake to California and back. He crossed the Sierras to Monterey and the following February, set out on the return trip. He followed

THE LONE LONE PINE PINE Historians say it was a tall Jeffrey Pine like the one at left that gave the area its name. An easy way to tell a Jeffrey from a Ponderosa Pine is by the spikes on the pine cones. A Jeffrey's curl in safely while a Ponderosa's stick out. Remember "gentle Jeffrey, prickly Ponderosa."

the Kern River out of the San Joaquin Valley, crossed the mountains over the pass named for him (down near Inyokern, east of Bakersfield) and swung North into what is now the Owens Valley.

But the Valley wasn't named on that trip, nor did Walker find any beaver, by the way. But he did discover Yosemite Valley and pioneered the Salt Lake-Humboldt trail, later a vital immigrant route.

In 1845, Captain John Fremont was still exploring the West and hired Walker to lead a mapping group south through the Valley. When the Mountain Man rejoined Fremont in San Jose, they talked of the grandeur of the mountains from the eastern side and of the large brackish alkaline lake Walker must have been accustomed to passing by now (he had been through there again as recently as 1843, guiding the Chiles wagons, which he had to abandon near the lake due to the exhaustion of the mules and the party being under-supplied [9])

As they worked on their maps, Fremont named that lake after one of his party's valuable hunters, Richard Owens. Ironically, Owens never saw the lake or the river, much less the valley, named after him.

fat hill

Southeast of Lone Pine, on the other side of the lake is the lively ghost town of Cerro Gordo[10] The name is Spanish for "Fat Hill," which undoubtedly had nothing to do with anything rotund but meant fat with silver[11]

Some Mexican prospectors (*Pablo Flores* is one of the names remembered) found silver here in 1865[12] and in its peak year, 1874, its three smelters turned out 5,300 tons of bullion worth $2,000,000. Its total production (well into this century) totalled $17,000,000. And it was to speed up the process of getting all that silver down to Los Angeles that something truly remarkable went on.

As hard as it is to look at the quiet and "empty" Alabama Hills today and envision literally hundreds of actors and horses and technicians scurrying like ants all over them, it is equally impossible

(for me, anyway) to drive by the parched Owens Dry Lake and picture boats chugging back and forth. Boats in the desert? You betcha.

The Owens Lake is (or was) the natural collection point for all the streams flowing into the Owens Valley. Before the Los Angeles Aqueduct (completed in 1913) diverted the river water, the lake covered 100 square miles and was at places 30 feet deep. And in the 1870's, today's tiny Cartago was a bustling port town!

The 85-foot *Bessie Brady* brought silver bullion from the Cerro Gordo mines to the landing at Cartago[13] where Remi Nadeau's celebrated 14 to 20-mule teams took it on down to Los Angeles. On the return trips, those freight wag-ons would bring food, grain, machinery, etc., up across the blistering Mojave for the mines.

Later, a second steamboat called the Molly.

2 From South to North: Mt. Langley, 14,062; Mt. Muir, 14,015; Mt. Russell, 14,086; Mt_Williamson, 14,375, and Mt. Tyndall, 14,018. Further North are Mt. Sill, 14,162, Split Mountain, 14,058, the Middle and North Palisades, 14,040 and 14,242, Mt. Sill, 14,162 and Thunderbolt Peak, also 14,040.

3 Study today's topographic maps. On the Lone Pine, Manzanar and Union Wash quadrangles, you can still see indications of tunnels and diggings in this section of the hills which extend north from Whitney Portal Road some five miles to the Alabama Gates, where they abruptly flatten out.

4 But some Yankee "one-ups-manship" was just around the corner. The next year, shortly after the Northern steam-sailer, the U.S.S. Kearsage, cornered and sank the Alabama off the coast of Normandy, gold in quartz veins was discovered west of Independence. Those prospectors were Northern sympathizers so they named not just their claims but a whole mining district, a mountain pass, a peak and a town "Kearsarger!"

5 It might even have been the "Hill party" which head quartered in the Lone Pine area the year before, doing exploratory mining.

6 Named after the county's first surveyor, Lyman Tuttle, according to Peter Browning in Place Names of the Sierra Nevada (1986, Wilderness Press, Berkeley).

7 Possibly in the severe 1861-62 winter when rainfall and snowfall reached record heights and all streams went roaring by, "always at flood stage," it was remembered. A year later, however, some similarly prominent tree was still being used as a landmark. The northern terminus of a trail-building project was described as being at 'a point in the Owens River Valley at the foot of the Big Meadows and the Lone Pine Tree.

8 For years, Jedediah Smith was credited with discovering the Valley when he crossed the Sierras west to east in 1826. But after discovering what is believed to be a copy of one of his maps — the originals disappeared when he was killed by Comanches — historians now believe he crossed the mountains farther north, near the present Ebbetts Pass.

9 See the excellent book, The California Trail, by George R. Stewart, one of the many historical works available at the Interagency Visitors Center at the Death Valley turn-off south of Lone Pine and at the Eastern California Museum up in Independence.

10 Renovation is currently underway of the several buildings remaining of what once was a collection of several separate mines (it was the Estelle that was used in Nevada Smith and you saw the general store at the beginning of Waterhole No. 3,) The area's Relshaw shaft goes down to 37 miles of tunnels (that's almost the driving distance from Olancha to Independence). To visit this lively old ghost town, contact Jodi Stewart or Mike Patterson for group tours (by reservation only) at 619-876-4154. And be warned: the road winding up to the old town rises 5,000 feet in that seven and a half miles. Four wheel drive vehicles are recommended.

11 So surmised Robert C. Likes and Glenn R. Day in their history of the mining area, Prom This Mountain — Cerro Gordo.

12 Friends of Flores would one day insist he had made his discovery earlier but couldn't do anything about it until the Indian troubles died down.

13 The first trips embarked from Swansea, where you can still see remnants of the wharf, originally made of slag and low grade ore from the mines.

Stevens also towed barges across the middle of the lake. And even those two boats have stories behind their names.

The *Bessie Brady* was built in 1872 by James Brady and named for his daughter who christened the new boat at Ferguson's Landing that July 4th.[14]

The next year, since the mines at Cerro Gordo needed wood and plenty of charcoal for its smelters, Colonel Sherman Stevens built a sawmill and flume in Cottonwood Canyon where trees were plentiful and shipped his lumber, mine timbers, etc. across the lake[15] first on barges behind the *Bessie Brady*, then later on the *Molly Stevens*, built in 1877 by Stevens and named after *his* daughter.

During this period, Olancha got into the act, too. It maintained large corrals for all those freight teams, which kept Cartago from clogging up. Some of those cottonwoods in Olancha, incidentally, were transplanted from Cottonwood Creek in the 1880's by a pioneer rancher to help make it the shady roadside stop it is today and *was* when it was a way station for the Owens Valley-Mojave stage.

a time of crime

Now we look at a time when the six-guns had real bullets in them.

Example — Before he moved south into the Los Angeles area toward the end of his career, one of California's most infamous bandit leaders, Tiburcio Vasquez,[16] ranged up and down the Owens Valley, holding up stages and freight wagons primarily around the mining camps southeast of the Lake. There was a time in 1874 when "Vasquez and his gang ruled the southern stage road and the highways of southern Inyo."[17]

Throughout the 1870's, there were shootings in Lone Pine and in the saloons of Cerro Gordo. The rowdies even invaded the courtrooms on occasion, once prompting District Judge Theron Y. Reed to spend the first day of court up the road in Independence shouting them down, or trying to. The next day was different. The next day, he brought a double-barreled shotgun to court — this was the *judge*, mind you; something right out of the Roy Bean handbook — and as he slowly cocked both barrels, he drily remarked, "Gentlemen, there will be order in this court today." And indeed there was.[18]

In 1878 and '79, two sheriffs died in shootings that read like scenes in the movies filmed here later — but they were tragically real. These men were pioneer settlers of the Valley, both of whom had taken part in the Indian wars, both of whom were leading citizens.

The first tragedy took place right in the town of Lone Pine, where you'll stay when you come to tour the Alabama Hills. A "hardened criminal" by the name of Palacio had murdered anIndian and when local citizens gave chase, he tried to hide in a drinking and gambling establishment run by a Frank Dabeeny, "another individual of the same stripe."[19]

Sheriff Thomas Passmore was called out from a sick bed and demanded entrance to Dabeeny's place, only to have those inside fire several shots through the door. The sheriff staggered back. "Boys, I'm shot," he exclaimed, then "handed his pistol to a bystander and fell dead."[20]

The crowd began riddling the building with gun-shots — this isn't a movie scene, don't forget; it really happened in 1878 — and when the men inside still refused to come out, there was talk of destroying the whole building if necessary to get them out. While they were deciding if it should be done by fire or dynamite (…dynamite??!),[21] a rider was sent up the road to Independence for help.

The siege was still underway when a big crowd rode in and that was when Palacio and Dabeeny tried to make a run for it. They didn't make it.

That sheriff was succeeded in office by W.L. Moore, nicknamed "Dad" because he was considered "the 'dad' of Lone Pine, having been one of its first residents." Up in Independence the following year for the Fourth of July celebration, he tried to stop a fight between two men by stepping between them when one of their guns went off. The bullet "passed through his watch, then through his body and he died in a few minutes."[22]

The gunman was captured immediately but the other man almost got away. They finally did find him, hiding under a house.

some 'firsts'

The first cattle were driven into the Valley in 1859 by L.R. Ketcham of Visalia. He left his stock near Lone Pine and rode on to the gold fields, then later sold his cattle at the Coso diggings.

In 1861, the McGee and Summers families drove cattle in from the Tulare Valley. The two boys, Bart and Alney McGee, decided to winter on Lone Pine Creek and were the first to build a cabin there.

The first white woman to settle in the Owens Valley was Mrs. Samuel Bishop. Her husband had brought in 500 cattle from Fort Tejon and although he spent only one season in the Valley, his name remains today on the creek where they made camp in August of 1861.

the indians and independence

That same month, Charles Putnam built a stone cabin along Little Pine creek. The trading post he established there is acknowledged as the beginning of what would become the town of Independence. But where did the name "Independence" come from? That story, too, has a natural progression.

As other homesteaders came into the grow-

Even settlers at Fort Independence made it on film. This time, the fort was built north of Horseshoe Meadow Road just beyond Rattlesnake Hill for *Song of The West*, 1930.

ing settlement, the first name change took place. The growing settlement they'd called merely Putnam's became Little Pine (after the creek). Then during that very hard winter of 1861-62, fights with the Paiutes began.

Hungry Indians butchered some cows, the settlers retaliated and a war was on, a war that would last a year and a half (but even as late as 1865, one pioneer family's diary recorded that "a horseman came rushing up and said that Indians had killed a woman and her son about 50 miles south of Lone Pine and were coming up the Valley."[23])

To protect the settlers, the Army established a garrison near Little Pine in the summer of 1862. The soldiers arrived on the Fourth of July and made camp along Oak Creek; you can still see the caves where they lived while putting up their buildings.[24] And as you have probably guessed, it was to commemorate their arrival on Independence Day that the new post was called ... Camp Independence.[25]

It was in 1866 that Little Pine changed its name to Independence on the occasion of the town becoming the county seat — which it still is.

But before the Army got there, that fight in the Alabama Hills took place.

The plan didn't work but the settlers were hoping that the Indians' cattle rustling could be nipped in the bud if a swift and decisive blow were struck at a main camp. In February of 1862, some two dozen settlers made a night march from Putnam's and at sunrise, attacked the Paiutes at a winter camp in the Alabama Hills, destroying much of their food reserves (more than a ton of dried meat).

This attack was probably out in the valley rocks (rather than in the rounded hills) because in describing the fight, pioneer Bart McGee wrote that when the Indians ran for shelter, they ducked into "cavities where they were out of sight in less than 30 seconds. (We shot) into the mouths of their dens while (they shot arrows at us) in showers...They did not have guns or they would have made a hard fight for us."

Think about that when you're out hiking in those same rocks.   And the sheriff getting shot through the door and those stagecoach hold-ups and the saloon shootings when next you're watching a Hopalong Cassidy.

The movie-makers maybe didn't know it but what they were doing had all happened before. For real. Right here.

[14] Its maiden voyage (carrying 30 tons of silver bullion) had been made eight days earlier.

[15] A touch over seven miles north of Cartago is a roadside marker on 395 telling about the still-standing charcoal kilns you can go visit down that dirt road. The Cottonwood landing was nearby.

[16] Coincidentally, another popular movie location, Vasquez Rocks (15 miles north of L.A.'s San Fernando Valley) was named after this bandit chief who supposedly hid out there during his latter years.

[17] W.A. Chalfant, *The Story of Inyo*, a book to buy and read.

[18] Ibid.

[19] Ibid.

[20] Ibid.

[21] They didn't use either and the building still stands. Today, it's the Indian Trading Post on the corner at the traffic signal. (That's the gift shop where all those Hollywood signatures are on the walls inside.)

[22] Ibid.

[23] Schumacher, *Deepest Valley*.

[24] Follow the map in the "OWENS VALLEY Guide to Independence and Lone Pine" by Helen Hoffman (maps and drawings by Ginna Jones). When you park at the old schoolhouse, go to the right of the worn sign across the road, then ease back to your left to get down to what hasn't washed away of the caves. (We mistakenly went down into the ravine to the right on our first visit and were forever finding them.)

[25] That 1872 earthquake destroyed most of the camp's original adobe buildings and the fort was rebuilt with wooden structures, many of them resembling the Mid-Western farmhouses the men had left years before. It thus was soon recognized as one of the most beautiful posts between St. Louis and San Francisco and when the camp was finally abandoned in 1877, at least two of the buildings, the Commander's House and the post hospital, were taken down and rebuilt in Independence, where you can still see them today. (Legend has it that the buildings were moved intact but that cannot be documented, according to Bill Michaels of the town's Eastern California Museum, a "must" place to visit, by the way.)

some tips on finding locations

see the 'simple' shot of roy rogers playing the guitar in 'under western stars'? Next, see what all it took to get that 'simple' shot? And look how many trucks were necessary for a location on 'song of the west.' The point is, when you're looking for a location, look for the road they needed to get there.

go find some yourself

Now it's your turn.

"The chase" was part of the fun in the old Westerns and it's part of the fun here, too, so go for it. Experience the thrill of the hunt.

So far, we've pinpointed the exact locations of many of the stills and scenes for you but there are other photos in the book we leave for you to find yourself. And if you don't find them on the first try, don't be disappointed; at least, you'll have earned yourself that steak dinner that night.

Also, of course, there are countless Lone Pine locations which aren't even in this book. So here are some suggestions for finding some of those — and by the way, what makes finding the locations possible today is not as much a clear photograph as it is the fact that the land, the rocks, the shapes are virtually unchanged since Fatty Arbuckle sat on that rock beside Tuttle Creek Road 70 years ago.

Sure, certain trees and clumps of sage might be bigger today (or gone entirely) but the rocks are the same, the mountain profiles are the same. But watch the roads. There's where you'll see the biggest difference. Roads that were okay to drive 50 years ago (or last year, for that matter) might have rain-washed gullies cutting across them now. So don't attempt driving that vehicle where you shouldn't. It's more fun walking those last few feet, anyhow.

Now those suggestions:

Suppose you're watching a video you've rented or bought of one of the Lone Pine movies and see the hero ride through some narrow pass with a pointed rock off to the side and you say, "Gee, I wonder where *that* is..."

If you don't already have a "still" of the scene (many people collect the old publicity photographs), then take or prepare your own.

Right off the television set.

Select one with as much landscape as possible, isolate it with your VCR's freeze-frame and make a sketch or take a Polaroid of the TV screen. (If you use a Polaroid, you don't always have to freeze-frame it; just don't shoot on a panning shot. You don't want to *add* movement — and remember to cover the flash with one hand.)

The ideal view is to have mountains in the background (specific shapes you can recognize) to give you your bearings, then middle distant rocks to line up on and foreground rocks to home in on. When you have three such coordinates, you're cookin'.

But be warned: many of those unchanged boulders tend to look like a lot of other unchanged boulders after awhile when you're out among 'em so if your scene has some rock with a distinctive shape or unique crack or hole or cleft, you're better off. And don't become confused if some of your terrain doesn't match other shots in the same scene. All angles in every scene were not always shot at the same location, remember. (Case in point: that *Lives of a Bengal Lancer* scene that began at Gary Coooper Rock and ended over near the Background Rocks.)

And don't be discouraged if you don't walk right to a particular location. We were nine hours finding that *Gunga Din* long shot at the left of page 70 (not all on one search, mind you, but spread out in two and three-hour hikes over three different trips to Lone Pine).

So just hang in there. There's always the next day. Or plan to spend your next vacation in Lone Pine, too. The rocks and the memories will always be there waiting for you.

You're on your own on these.

WHEN POSSIBLE when you're looking for locations, first look for recognizable landmarks in the photos, like the circled group of Three Rocks (called by some the Buttons) in these two shots from 1935's "Lives of a Bengal Lancer. They're part of that rock cluster on the Horseshoe Meadow Road which holds the Temple Pocket (and can also be seen in that "Yellow Sky" photo on page 39, among others). In the photo above, those two rock columns behind Gary Cooper appear to be sharp-pointed so you can look for those against the cliffs (one clue: this is near the "Yellow Sky" arrastra). In the photo to the right, you have the mountain line and the big rock hill to guide on, so line up the Buttons to the other landmarks and go get 'em!

and the search goes on

Yes, the search goes on, the continued search for movie memories out in those Movie Rocks.

Pushing through the sage, looking for the exact locations where scenes were shot, poring through shoe-boxes in a Lone Pine attic or down in L.A., looking for photos taken when Hollywood was making all those movies out there - - that's what keeps you hopping. Plus (and perhaps this is the most important task historically) continuing the search for the names of the movies shot "on location in Lone Pine."

When this book was first published in 1990 - just in time for the first Lone Pine Film Festival -- it listed 150 films. The revised 2005 edition added more than 200 titles. This edition includes yet another 89 titles.

The discovery of many of them was the work of a former Lone Pine school teacher named Chris Langley who became a Man with a Mission. He's the one who haunted the nostalgia movie shops in New York and L.A., questioned fellow film historians and collectors, examined old Owens Valley newspapers and pored through all those photos and lobby cards and posters at collectors' shows and on the Internet. Since Holly and I moved back into the Los Angeles area in 2003 (after 12 glorious years in Lone Pine; to be closer to the "kids"), Chris became Keeper of the Flame. He is Inyo County's Film Commissioner, has authored several books on the area and still keeps the movie list current.

Don't forget the criteria for a film to make that list: all of its exteriors needn't have been shot here, as they were pretty much for 1948's Yellow Sky, for instance. No, even if just parts of a picture were filmed here, it counts. The test question is a simple one: Did they come to Lone Pine to film? That way, even those brief chase scenes in The Rawhide Years (1956) with Tony Curtis got that one on the list. In fact, just one shot will do it, like when we saw the balloon over the Alabama Hills at the end of Around the World In 80 Days (1956). And if a company headquartered here so they could shoot nearby, that works, too, as was the case with 1994's Terminal Velocity. They ate and slept and made their plans here but actually shot over in Saline Valley on the way to Death Valley; that's where they dropped that car out of the airplane.

adding new titles

Who'd have thought that movie tough guy Alan Ladd -- he of those exotic locales (China, Saigon, Calcutta) - would have roughed it in Lone Pine! But look at 1953's Desert Legion and there he is, first out in the sand dunes down at Olancha as a Legionnaire, then with Tony Caruso and Akim Tamaroff (riding camels no less) in the easily recognizable Temple Pocket1 off Horseshoe Meadow Road.

And remember Charlton Heston's Ben Hur (1959) and the terrific and always moving Best Years of Our Lives (1946)? No, I'm not claiming them as Lone Pine pictures but since this book first came out, we did learn that their director, William Wyler, was here, back in the silent days when he was learning his trade doing two-reel Westerns at Universal. He directed Blazing Days, The Stolen Ranch, The Horse Trader and The Square Shooter out in our rocks and was the first assistant on The Gold Trap and Taking Chances, among others we're still trying to verify.[2]

There are some great Wyler/ Lone Pine stories in a new Wyler biography.[3] One has him trudging back into Lone Pine after a long day's shoot in the rocks, then driving six hours down to L.A. to see a girlfriend for a couple of hours, then six hours back to be on the set at 8 a.m.!

The point of the story is not the idiocy of youth but that while that's a three-and-a-half to four hour drive nowadays, in the '20's, it took six. (I would have thought more.) His passion gave us new movie making information about the early days.[4]

William Wyler's pictures won 38 Academy Awards, twice as many as any other director. And he cut his teeth in Lone Pine.

a lone pine fire

Another book to look for[5] is one about Father John J. Crowley, a forceful and influential community and spiritual leader for years in the Owens Valley and Death Valley areas. Among many movie stories in it is one about a big Lone Pine fire that took place two nights after Errol Flynn and David Niven got to town.6

Tantalizing excerpts from a Father Crowley newspaper column the author shared with us tell how he was on the roof of the church7 hosing it down to protect it, etc. To get more details, we went to the newspaper archives in the Laws Railroad Museum and Historical Site north of Bishop.

It was early Wednesday morning, April 1, 1936, and as reported in Bishop's Inyo Register of April 2: "fire swept away the Mt. Whitney Cafe and Ellis Motors in Lone Pine soon after midnight Tuesday.

"A Warner Brothers motion picture unit comprising about 240 persons is in Lone Pine filming scenes for 'The Charge of the Light Brigade,' a forthcoming big production. The cafe expected to serve breakfast for the company yesterday morning and to be ready for an early hour, left an oil-burning range turned on. An overflow of oil occurred and ignited. . . . When the fire department responded to call, the new hose they unreeled would not fit the nearest hydrant . . "By the time it was taken to another hydrant and a connection made, it is said 45 minutes had elapsed. By then, the building was beyond saving.

"Ellis Motors, next south, contained 11 new Ford cars, which were all taken out safely. That building and much of its contents went the same way as the cafe. 8

"Heat from the fire broke windows of the

Lone Pine Lumber Company building across the street."⁹

That day, costumes and props had been handed out to the Warner Brothers cast (which filled the Dow Hotel) and the April 3rd *Inyo Independent* reported that "The alarm was given throughout the Hotel by bugles." It also added that "the fire engine was immediately called but no one knew how to operate it (at first)."

The Independent went on to say that when 'phone service was interrupted (two 'phone poles by Ellis Motors were burning), "immediate connections were made for the Dow Hotel and all telegrams and telephone calls were cared for through courtesy of the Dow Hotel."

Father Crowley's column noted that a radio news report out of Salt Lake City said "The members of the cast of "The Charge of the Light Brigade," starring Errol Flynn, now on location in that town, battled heroically with the flames."

None of the reports said where they finally got breakfast.¹⁰ But another article did say that 43 members of the company were staying at the Winnedumah Hotel in Independence and in order for them to get down to Lone Pine in time to start work with everyone else, they had their breakfasts served at 4 a.m. every morning.

care for seconds?

Moving right along, it was not unusual for big-time "A" pictures to send second units up here so they could include just the right terrain. And the new titles verify that.

A guy was in Lone Pine's video store one day and said, "Y'all don't have *Ox-Bow Incident* on your list of Lone Pine movies." The clerk passed on the comment and I almost laughed. I hadn't watched the Henry Fonda classic in years but I could easily remember the sound stage hanging and the street stuff on the back-lot. Nothing out in our rocks. I would have bet your house on it.

But it had been years so I dug it out and sure

Bugles awakened the Light Brigade cat and crew one night; a big fire across the street! Here are Patric Knowles, left and Errol Flynn out on Movie Road the next day.

enough, there they were.

Director William Wellman had indeed sent up a second unit to show the posse heading into the mountains. No principals, just long shots but there they were, first in the Alabams, then heading up toward Mt. Whitney. So much for memory. You always have to check. (And who knows, maybe that footage inspired Wellman to come here in person to shoot *Yellow Sky*.)

There were even a couple of Lone Pine shots in the 1992 *Chaplin*! A second unit was here with some old flivvers doing chase scenes along Movie Road, a second unit directed by Mickey Moore, whose career also dated back to the silents. He was a child actor with Tom Mix!

Even the renowned Cecil B. DeMille sent a second unit here for *Samson and Delilah* (doubles for Victor Mature and Hedy Lamarr racing along in that chariot just before the lion gets killed). And the new list reveals that no less than Alfred Hitchcock also sent a second unit to Lone Pine.

It was for the bit in 1942's *Saboteur* where Priscilla Lane and a hand-cuffed Robert Cummings are driving along and she escapes and is trying to flag down help. Watch for it on TV. You'll see them along Whitney Portal Road west of Horseshoe and you'll swear the doubles are Lane and Cummings. That's the fun of Hollywood magic.

1   So-called, you remember, because that's where RKO built the Temple of Kali for Gunga Din. And just off the road is the Gunga Din Marker that Douglas Fairbanks, Jr. dedicated when he was here.
2   Thunder Riders (1927) and Shootin' Irons (1927).
3   Putnam's "A Talent for Trouble" by Jan Herman.
4   But that drive time's nothing compared to the really "old days." An April, 1875, issue of The Inyo Independent said that the "time of the Southern Stage Line from Lone Pine to Los Angeles is 48 hours, fare $40."
5   "The Desert Padre" by Joan Brooks.
6   The Inyo Independent reported that the company headed up to Lone Pine Monday, March 30, 1936, but was "delayed a number of hours because the train ran out of water and had to go to Trona for a new supply." Director Michael Curtiz and Director of Photography Sol Polito came up a day earlier.
7   At the time, the Catholic church was where the parking lot and swimming pool of the Dow Villa Motel are today. In the column Ms. Brooks sent, Father Crowley wrote of "skating" up there because although it was early April, the water froze as it hit the roof!

more?

What other names and stories do the new additions reveal? You may now include Sir Richard Burton among the many distinguished actors who toiled out in our Movie Rocks. The one-time Elizabeth Taylor husband played Edwin Booth here in *Prince of Players*, while the long-time Taylor companion, Roddy McDowall, was here in 1949 with a dear friend of Lone Pine's and the Festival's, Rand Brooks,[11] in a picture for Lindsley Parsons. who wrote so many of John Wayne's Lone Star Westerns.

A pre-*Stagecoach* Claire Trevor was here for a George O'Brien Western and a post-*Bewitched* Elizabeth Montgomery was here as TV's *Mrs. Sundance*. And Richard Dix (whose *Cimarron* was the first Western to win a Best Picture Oscar) was here with Preston Foster for the 1940 re-make of the first picture done in Lone Pine. *The Round-Up* and Dix returned for *Tombstone, The Town Too Tough To Die*.

always learning

A local packer named Henry Olivas once told the Chamber of Commerce he remembered packing Tom Forman up to Horseshoe Meadows in the early '20s to do *The Virginian*. Forman was an actor of the period so that made sense; he was even in Lone Pine's first movie with Fatty Arbuckle, 1920's *The Round-Up*. So when we came across a *Virginian* released in 1923, we got excited, then confused.

We fast-forwarded into the picture to check out the backgrounds and it wasn't Forman in the starring role, it was Kenneth Harlan! (The same Harlan who 15 or 20 years later would be playing such character roles as a good banker in a Hoppy[12] and an unscrupulous one in an Eliiott[13]). But then we went back and read the credits and "Leakey" Olivas was vindicated. Forman wasn't in that *Virginian*, he directed it!

What else have we learned as we added titles to the list? We generally remember Guinn "Big Boy" Williams as the rough - housing teddy bear of a sidekick to such stars as Errol Flynn, Robert Mitchum, even Roy Rogers, but there was a time early on when he starred in Westerns and two of those were done here.

Even famous songs were introduced here! In MGM's *The Firefly* (1937), Allan Jones (Jack Jones' father) sings "Donkey Serenade" to none other than Jeannette MacDonald as she's riding in a coach and he's horseback alongside.

In the movie as seen in the theaters, you only see them against a rear projection screen and you think, "Well, just the coach was up here for the long shots" but come to find out, they did film the song here; they just didn't use the footage.

Jones sang to playback as he rode alongside the coach over in Tuttle Creek Canyon. Another long-time resident, Mat Perez, was working on a road crew at the time and watched them shoot it.

"maverick"

Speaking of footage shot but not used, that all but sums up the Lone Pine visit of the *Maverick* company. The 1994 film spent weeks here, most of that time spent constructing, then shooting in and around a split-level "cabin" set that Tom Sanders[14] designed and built into the rocks. In the story, actress Linda Hunt used bits and pieces discarded by passing wagon trains to build this wonderful rambling makeshift affair, complete with suspension bridges to sun decks with nearby corrals for cows and sheep, etc.

After Maverick's near-hanging,[15] he recuperates there and Hunt (as a character called 'The Magician') shares the wisdom of the ages with him. Not one foot of the extensive footage made it into the finished film.

You still see Mount Whitney in other shots, there are scenes with Mel Gibson, James Garner and Jodie Foster shot on the slopes of the Sierras just off Whitney Portal Road, the Indian-wagon train stuff was shot near Manzanar and Big Pine (did you spot Margot Kidder?) and James Coburn came up for those campfire scenes at the end, so *Maverick* was certainly a legitimate addition to the list. But no rock shots.

Actually, how they came to shoot here at all is interesting.

In June of 1993, I was asked to take director Richard Donner and his location people and production design people on a scout of the

---

8 In 1936, Ellis Motors was where Lone Pine Rocks and Gifts is today at the NW corner of 395 and Post. The Mt. Whitney Cafe was where it is today. The rebuilding of both burned buildings began two weeks after the fire. (Ellis Motors would eventually move further south to where "The Building" (formerly the old Schat's Bakery Building) is now at the corner of 395 and Tim Holt Street, subsequently changing its name to Eastern Sierra Motors and later moving to Bishop.)
9 Where the new hostel is today.
10 But we did find other fascinations. At the Sterling Garage, Lone Pine's Chevrolet dealership (located where the Pizza Factory is today), a new Chevy coupe was $495. At Lone Pine's Safeway Market, coffee was 15 cents a pound, bacon 29 cents. And on May 31, 1936, the completion by the CCC of "a good mountain road" up to Hunter's Flat was dedicated and "a small lake is being created just below the falls." (That's the lake Hoppy and California ride by in 1940's *Three Men From Texas*.) And the name of Hunter's Flat was changed to - - you guessed it - - Whitney Portal.
11 "Lucky" in the last dozen Hoppys, eight of which were shot in Lone Pine.

Sherman To Film In Lone Pine: Fox Co. Leaves

Lone Pine and vicinity continued to hum this week with motion picture location activity as two companies departed for Hollywood headquarters and another moved in to shoot western pictures. Republic studio company returned late last week after spending nine days filming John Kimbrough and Shiela Ryan and subordinates in "Lone Star Ranger." Numerous Lone Pine residents were included in the picture, while many street scenes were taken in the business section.

Harry Sherman and a large group arrived in Lone Pine this week to begin filming a Richard Dix picture. Early reports were that the name of the film will be "Tombstone."

INYO INDEPENDENT
August 29, 1941

Alabama Hills. They were flying in from Oregon, travelling the West, selecting *Maverick* locations.

A doctor's appointment I just couldn't cancel prevented my going on that first scout so our son Michael (who had just graduated from high school here) met them at the airport and guided the three car caravan out into the rocks.

Knowing that Donner was an avid movie buff and historian (that's why he's such a good director; he's just a plain out-and-out fan like us), I suggested to Michael that "when you're finished showing them what they want to see, do like I do on these movie scouts: offer to show them some of the movie sites out there," where classic scenes were shot over the years. Movie people love that sort of thing. "Make sure they're done working for the day," I cautioned, "then ask if they have time to 'play' some before leaving."

The story is finished in the official 19 pages of production notes that Warner Brothers sent out in all the press packets publicizing the film.

"Director Donner recalls the first time he saw the area", the press book reports. "The local historian (sic) took me to a rock, " Donner said, "and there on this rock was a piece of cement and a metal tube. And he said this is where the strut of the bridge was that Cary Grant was crossing when the elephant tried to come on behind him in 'Gunga Din.' My heart stopped." (*Gunga Din* is Donner's favorite movie.) "We had to shoot there!" The past really is prologue.

The Alabama Hills being so spectacular, Donner probably would have shot here even without the history lesson. But that sure cinched it.

the shadow's shadow

Michael Holland appears in another footnote to Lone Pine's movie story.

He was home from college and working as a production assistant with the company that had come up to do *The Shadow*.

The scouting was complete, the exterior sets were built and they had finally finished wiring the faux opium poppies and leaves onto two or three acres of sagebrush to simulate that big poppy field you see at the beginning of the picture. It was time for the main company to drive up for the actual filming.

As Fate would have it, they were set to leave Universal super early on Monday, January 17, 1994, the day of that disastrous earthquake in Los Angeles' San Fernando Valley. Around 4 a.m. when the quake struck, some of the cars and trucks had just cleared the Newhall Pass heading North, barely making it out of the Valley. But most did not.

Star Alec Baldwin didn't make it up, neither did director Russell Mulcahy. The Director of Photography, Steve Burum, was in the first car so he did get through but many of his assistants did not and Burum kept joking under his breath, "Hope I remember how to load film."

Since the director didn't make it to Lone Pine, the first assistant, Louis D'Esposito, took over. And since Alec Baldwin couldn't come up, they needed someone to double him in the scene where the bad guys are taking a kidnapped Lamont Cranston to the Holy Man's Temple.

"Who can we get up here that rides horseback?" they asked Michael.

"I can," he said and that's how he came to be in *The Shadow*, doubling Baldwin as they ride toward camera between those columns of flags. Since Michael's hands were supposedly tied behind his back, his horse was led at a gallop by a costumed local cowboy, Leonard Watterson, and he was flanked by two other locals, Tom Noland[16] and Lee Roeser.[17] They pulled Michael off the horse so he could magically become Alec Baldwin in the close-up. I love movies.

"iron men" in the old west

One of the great things when talking about the movies they make here is, simply, that they're still making them. And two great examples of that are 2008's *Iron Man* and 2012's *Django Unchained*.

These are two powerhouse A-listers, with the likes of Robert Downey Jr., Jon Favreau, Quentin Tarantino, Christoph Waltz and Jamie Foxx working here. (These talents after, remember, Ridley Scott and Russell Crowe here in 2000's *Gladiator*. And, sure, some of 2013's *The Lone Ranger* was done out on the Owens dry lake.) Point is, Hollywood still loves to get out and play on location.

In the opening moments of *Iron Man*, the view is unmistakably our Alabama Hills with the Sierras in the back. Tony Stark is discussing his weapons with some soldiers (GPS Extra 2). To impress them, he introduces his Jericho missile for an explosive result. Chris Langley was out with the crew during filming and tells of the crew calling this area the "bombing area". Yep, this is how locations get names! Anyway, we know it as an Audie Murphy location (GPS Extra 1). Audie's friend has been chained to a rock in Showdown, one of the three separate quality B-westerns he did in these hills. Again, two movies made in the same area but years apart!

Actually, there's some great Behind The Scenes footage on the *Iron Man* DVD of their shooting in the rocks and out in the Olancha sand dunes. Favreau says getting to Lone Pine "was well worth it because it really gives you a look like we traveled halfway around the world." And Downey Jr. says, "What a privilege it was to be able to be there playing this guy with the caliber of people I was working with. What a blast."

And why did Tarantino – film buff that he is – want to shoot *Django Unchained* in Lone Pine? Because this is where a favorite of his, William Witney, had worked! As Tarantino told The New York Times in 2000, "People think that the only good westerns made in the 40s and 50s were by John Ford or maybe Howard Hawks. Film guys might add Anthony Mann, Budd Boetticher and Andre De Toth but William Witney is ahead of them all; the one whose movies I can show to anyone and they are just blown away." Tarantino even used one of

---

12 *Range War* (1939).
13 *Prairie Schooners* (1940).
14 Also production designer of Coppola's *Bram Stoker's Dracula* and art director on Spielberg's *Hook,* among many others.
15 Filmed at both the El Mirage Dry Lake near Victorville (where the Stagecoach Indian chase was shot) and here on the northern-edge mud flats of our own Owens Dry Lake, accessed east of the train depot.

Witney's original clappers – the slate you see at the beginning of each shot that lists the Scene & Take and shows Sync – on the film.

Which brings us to our Lone Pine Film History Museum. Tarantino frequented the place, including – to share his love of cinema as he often does – screening old westerns in The Museum's Theatre for his cast & crew. And when shooting wrapped, he graciously donated Schultz' dentist's wagon to The Museum. And what else?

Well, in true Lone Pine movie making tradition, Tarantino & Cast signed their autographs right on a wall! (Now where have we seen this before?)[26]

So where did they film, you ask? As Django and fellow slaves' iron chains ring through the desert rocks in the opening scene (GPS Extra 4), you'll recognize the Alabams all right. But you might not realize, in the background, you're looking at Gene Autry Rock at a different angle! And Dr. King Shultz and Django's campsite (GPS Extra 3)? Yep, in Lone Ranger Canyon, where Witney shot that '38 Serial.

The GPS coordinates for these new locations are referenced in our new GPS chart!

the film festival

Since 1990 all that movie heritage has been celebrated each year at the popular Lone Pine Film Festival.

Some 5,000 fans come from as far away as Great Britain, South America, Canada and all over the U.S., including the East Coast (New York, Pennsylvania, the Carolinas, etc.) to meet stars who worked here, see movies that were made here[18] and take bus-and-walking tours[19] of actual movie locations out in the Alabama Hills where photos are set up to mark exactly where scenes were shot.

Held every October on Columbus Day weekend, the Festival has seen such favorites as Roy Rogers, Clayton Moore and Douglas Fairbanks, Jr. here to meet the fans in person. (That's right; the King of the Cowboys, the Lone Ranger and Sergeant Ballantine all here in person! Gregory Peck even came up one weekend!)

Other guest stars (listed alphabetically) have included John Agar, Budd Boetticher, Ernest Borgnine, Grace Boyd, Ben Burtt, Rand Brooks, Pat Buttram, Harry Carey Jr., Dick Jones, Burt Kennedy, Leonard Maltin, Virginia Mayo, George Montgomery, Ann Rutherford, Walter Reed, Peggy Stewart, Ruth Terry, Mrs. John (Pilar) Wayne, William Wellman Jr., and Republic director William Witney - - not to mention such stuntmen as the great Joe Yrigoyen, Jack Williams, Henry Wills and Loren Janes (who doubled Steve McQueen his entire 22-year career). And those who appeared in our Friday night concerts: Eddie Dean, Rex Allen, Roy Rogers Jr. (Dusty Rogers), The Reinsmen, The Sons of the San Joaquin, The Lobo Rangers, Rusty Richards, the American Cowboys, Dave Stamey, RW Hampton and Belinda Gail to name a few. A detailed list is available on the festivals website www.lonepinefilmfestival.org.

You'll often see such hero look-alikes as Joe Sullivan as Hoppy, Don Shilling as Paladin and Bill Nohl as Roy Rogers in the Sunday parade with the guest stars and local bands and such. There's a big arts and crafts show in the park. In town, look for the building where vendors make memories available to take home: videos, books, posters and lobby cards, etc. and stars will autograph their photos and books. You can take horseback rides and wagon rides along those happy trails out in that living museum.[20] And almost every year, a bronze plaque is dedicated and put up somewhere to designate movie points of interest.[21]

Some say the most fun is the Saturday morning question-and-answer panel discussion with the stars. And talk about the stories!

Grace Boyd told so many: how Hoppy was making a movie here in Lone Pine when he returned to L.A. so they could get married, how she was the one who named Topper, how she used to have a bubble bath and a glass of wine waiting for Bill in their room back at the Dow after a blistering day in the Alabams. "Close that transom," he cautioned in that wonderful deep voice. "If anyone should see this . . ."

Dick Farnsworth (the "Grey Fox" himself) remembered cooling off after doubling Guy Madison

continued on page 97

The author with Clayton Moore, Douglas Fairbanks, Jr. and Rand Brooks at the 1992 Film Festival.

---

16 Manager of the local Anchor Ranch.
17 He and his wife run the McGee Creek Pack Station.

all the films ... so far

listed alphabetically for easy reference

26 Men: Incident at Yuma	1957	Beyond the Purple Hills	1950	Call of the Canyon	1942	Destry	1954
3 Godfathers	1948	Beyond the Rockies	1932	Cameraman, The	1920	Devil's Playground, The	1946
5 Million Footsteps	2004	Bicyclist, The	1994	Cattle Empire	1958	Digital Man	1995
Across The Plains	1928	Big Timber	1950	Cattle Thief, The	1936	Dinosaur	2000
Across the Plains	1939	Black Jack	1927	Chaplin	1992	Django Unchained	2012
Adventures of Captain Marvel	1941	Black Midnight	1949	Charge of the Light Brigade, The	1936	Doolins of Oklahoma, The	1949
Adventures in Wild California	2000	Blackjack Ketchum, Desperado	1956	Chasing Trouble	1926	Down Mexico Way	1941
Adventures of Champion, The	1955	Blazing Days	1927	Cheyenne: The Travelers	1956	Dudes Are Pretty People	1942
Adventures of Hajji Baba, The	1954	Blazing Sun, The	1950	Cimarron Strip	1967	Durand of the Bad Lands	1925
Adventures of Marco Polo, The	1938	Blue Steel	1934	Cisco Kid and the Lady, The	1939	Dynamite Pass	1950
Alias Smith and Jones	1971	Bonanza, The Pursued: Part 1	1966	Clean-Up Man, The	1928	Eagle's Feather, The	1923
Along the Great Divide	1951	Bonanza, The Pursued: Part 2	1966	Clearing the Trail	1928	Enchanted Hill, The	1926
And I Alone Survived	1978	Boots and Saddles	1937	Code of the West	1947	Escape in the Desert	1945
Annie Oakley	1954	Border Cavalier, The	1927	Colt Comrades	1943	Everyman's Law	1936
Arizona Cyclone, The	1928	Border Treasure	1950	Comanche Station	1960	Eye For An Eye, An (aka Talion)	1966
Arizona Ranger, The	1948	Border Vigilantes	1941	Comin' Round the Mountain	1936	Fair Warning	1931
Army Girl	1938	Born to the Saddle	1953	Coral Reef Adventure	2003	False Colors	1943
Army of One	1993	Born to the West	1937	Counting Sheep	2004	False Paradise	1948
Around the World	1943	Borrowed Trouble	1948	Courageous Avenger, The	1935	Farewell to Manzanar	1976
Around the World in 80 Days	1956	Bounty	2002	Cow Town	1950	Fiddlin' Buckaroo, The	1933
Autry AMC's Documentary	1994	Brass Commandments	1923	Cowboy and the Lady, The	1938	Fighting Fury	1924
Back Trail, The	1924	Brick Bradford	1947	Cowboy Holiday	1934	Fighting Legion, The	1930
Bad Day at Black Rock	1955	Bridger	1976	Crash and Burn	1990	Firefly	2002
Bad Lands, The	1925	Brigham Young Frontiersman	1940	Crooked River	1950	Firefly, The	1937
Bad Man, The	1930	Brimstone	1949	Crossworlds	1996	Flame of Araby	1951
Baghdad	1949	Broken Arrow	1950	Cupid the Cowpuncher	1920	Flaming Guns	1932
Bamboo Saucer, The	1968	Bruce Gentry	1949	Daft Punk's Electroma	2006	Flying Horseman, The	1926
Bar 20	1943	Brute, The	1927	Danger Trials	1935	Fool's Gold	1946
Bar 20 Rides Again	1935	Buffalo Bill, Jr.: The Black Ghost	1955	Dangerous Venture	1947	For Those We Love	1921
Barbary Coast Gent	1944			Daredevils of the West	1943	Freighters of Destiny	1931
Barbed Wire	1952	Bug	2007	Daring Chances	1924	Friend of the Devil	2009
Between Fighting Men	1932	Caged Fury	1990	Dark Rider	1991	From Hell to Texas	1958
Between Men	1935			Dead Don't Dream, The	1948	Frontier Days	1934
				Death Falls	1991	Frontier Marshal	1939
				Death Valley Gunfighter	1949	G.I. Jane	1997
				Demon For Trouble, A	1934	G.I. Joe - The Rise of the Cobra	2009
				Demon, The	1926		
				Desert Hawk, The	1950	Gay Caballero, The	1940
				Desert Legion	1953	Gene Autry Show, The	1950
				Desert Pursuit	1952	Ghost of Zorro	1949

Girl-Shy Cowboy	1928
Gladiator	2000
Gold Trap, The	1925
Golden Princess, The	1925
Goldtown Ghost Riders	1953
Gone in Sixty Seconds	2000
Good Bye, Guy Guy	2002
Grail, The	1923
Great Race, The	1965
Greed	1924
Gun Gospel	1927
Gun Law	1938
Gun Smugglers	1948
Gunfighter, The	1950
Gunfire at Indian Gap	1957
Gunga Din	1939
Guns of Hate	1948
Gunsmoke Ranch	1937
Hallelujah Trail, The	1965
Hands Across the Border	1944
Hands Off	1927
Hangman's Knot	1952
Have Gun - Will Travel	1957
Heart of Arizona	1938
Heart of the Golden West	1942
Hell Bent for Leather	1960
Hell-Fire Austin	1932
Hey! Hey! Cowboy	1927
Hidden Valley	1932
High Sierra	1941
Highway 395	2000
Hills of Utah, The	1951
Hired Gun, The	1957
Hitchhiker, The	1953
Hi-Yo Silver	1940
Hollywood Cowboy	1937
Homer and Eddie	1989
Hop-A-Long Cassidy (Enters)	1935
Hopalong Cassidy: Public Hero #1	2001
Hopalong Rides Again	1937
Hoppy Serves A Writ	1943
Horse Trader, The	1927
Hot News	1928
How the West Was Won	1962
I Cover the War	1937
I Died a Thousand Times	1955
In Old Colorado	1941
In Old Monterey	1939
Indian Agent	1948
Iron Man	2008
Jack Armstrong	1947
Joe Kidd	1972
Jonathan Livingston Seagull	1973
Jouer Sa Vie (The Great Chess Movie)	1982
Jungle Raiders	1945
Just Tony	1922
Kalifornia	1993
Kim	1950
King of the Khyber Rifles	1953
King of the Pecos	1936
Knights of the Range	1940
Last Musketeer, The	1952
Last of the Duanes, The	1941
Last of the Pony Riders	1953
Last Place on Earth, The	2002
Last Posse, The	1953
Law and Jake Wade, The	1958
Law and Lead	1936
Law of the Pampas	1939
Lawless Range	1935
Lawless Riders	1935
Leather Burners	1943
Letters from Moab, The	1991
Life in the Raw	1933
Light of Western Stars, The	1940
Lightning Bryce	1919
Little Eden	2003
Lives of a Bengal Lancer, The	1935
Llano Kid, The	1939
Loaded Pistols	1948
Lone Ranger, The	1938
Lone Ranger, The	2013
Lone Star Ranger	1942
Lonely Man, The	1957
Long, Long Trailer, The	1953
Lost Horizon	1937
Loves of Carmen, The	1948
Lucky Terror	1936
Man from Music Mountain	1943
Man From Utah, The	1934
Man From Wyoming, The	1924
Man in the Saddle	1951
Man of Steel	2013
Man Who Won, The	1923
Man's Country	1938
Masked Raiders	1949
Master of the World	1961
Maverick	1994
Melody Ranch	1940
Men In the Raw	1923
Men of the Timberland	1941
Mighty Treve, The	1937
Mine with the Iron Door, The	1924
Money, Women and Guns	1958
Monolith Monsters The	1957
Moonlight on the Prairie	1935
Mrs. Sundance	1974
Mule Train	1950
Mysterious Desperado, The	1949
Mystery Man	1944
Nevada	1944
Nevada Smith	1966
Nevadan, The	1950
New Age, The	1994
New Frontier, The	1935
North to Alaska	1960
Oh, Susanna!	1936
Oil for the Lamps of China	1935
Old Barn Dance, The	1938
Old Oklahoma Plains	1952
One Mad Kiss	1930
Oregon Trail, The	1936
Outlaws of the Desert	1941
Outlaws of the Orient	1937
Ox-Bow Incident, The	1943
Panhandle	1948
Panic in Motion	2005
Pardon My Gun	1930
Perfect	1985
Phantasm 4 aka Oblivion	1998
Phantom of the Range, The	1936
Pirates On Horseback	1941
Plainsman and the Lady	1946
Points West	1929
Pollyanna	1920
Posse From Hell	1961
Postman, The	1997
Pride of the West	1938
Prince of Players	1955
Prospector, The	1998
Prowlers of the Night	1926
Rambling Ranger, The	1927
Range Rider, The	1951
Range War	1939
Ranger of the North	1927
Rat Race	2001
Rawhide	1951
Rawhide Years, The	1955
Red Blood and Blue	1925
Red Rider, The	1925
Red Ryder	1951
Red Shadow, The	1932
Red Warning, The	1923
Renegade Trail	1939
Replikator	1994
Republic Pictures Story	1991
Resurrection	2004
Return of Jack Slade, The	1955
Rhythm on the Range	1936
Ride Clear of Diablo	1954
Ride Lonesome	1959

Rider from Tucson	1950
Rider of the Law	1927
Rider of the Pass, The	1925
Riders from Tucson	1950
Riders of the Dawn	1937
Riders of the Deadline	1943
Riders of the Frontier	1939
Riders of the Purple Sage	1925
Riders of the Purple Sage	1941
Riders of the Sand Storm	1925
Ridin' Kid from Powder River, The	1924
Ridin' Rascal, The	1926
Ridin' Romance	1926
Rip Roarin' Buckaroo	1936
Roaring West, The	1935
Romance of the Rio Grande	1941
Rootin' Tootin' Rhythm	1937
Rough and Ready	1927
Round Up, The	1920
Round Up, The	1940
Running On The Sun	2000
Rustler's Roundup	1933
Saboteur	1942
Saga of Death Valley	1939
Salome Where She Danced	1945
Salt Lake Trail	1926
Samson and Delilah	1949
Sand	1949
Sand Trap	1998
Sandflow	1937
Savage Dawn	1985
Secret Valley	1937
Secrets of the Wasteland	1941
Senor Daredevil	1926
Seven Men From Now	1956
Shadow, The	1994
Shootin' Irons	1927
Showdown	1963
Silent Conflict	1948
Silent Rider, The	1928
Sinister Journey	1948
Six Shootin' Romance, A	1926
Sky King	1951
Slow Burn	2000
Smokey Smith	1936
Somewhere In Sonora	1927
Somewhere In Sonora	1933
Song of Nevada	1944
Song of Texas	1943
Song of the West	1930
Splitting the Breeze	1927
Sporting West	1925
Springfield Rifle	1952
Spurs	1930
Square Shooter, The	1927
Stage to Tucson	1950
Stagecoach Kid	1949
Stand Up for Justice	2004
Star Is Born, A	1937
Star Trek Generations	1995
Star Trek V: The Final Frontier	1989
Star Trek: Enterprise, Fight or Flight	2001
Sting of the Lash	1921
Stolen Ranch, The	1926
Storm Over Bengal	1938
Strange Gamble	1948
Stranger Wore A Gun, The	1953
Sundown Jim	1942
Sunset Pass	1946
Sunset Trail, The	1924
Superman	1948
Sweet Poison	1991
Swiss Movements	1927
Taking Chances	1925
Tall T, The	1957
Taming Power of the Small	1995
Tarzan's Desert Mystery	1943
Tarzan's Savage Fury	1952
Terminal Velocity	1994
Terror Trail	1933
Texans Never Cry	1951
Texas Across The River	1966
Texas Bad Man, The	1932
Texas Trail	1937
Three Faces West	1940
Three Godfathers, The	1948
Three Men from Texas	1940
Three On The Trail	1936
Thunder in the Sun	1959
Thunder Mountain	1947
Thunder Riders	1928
Thundering Herd, The	1933
Timegate	1972
Tombstone, The Town Too Tough To Die	1942
Toyo Miyatake: Infinite Shades of Gray	2001
Trail of the Vigilantes	1940
Trail To San Antone	1947
Trailin' Trouble	1930
Transformers: Revenge of the Fallen	2009
Trapped	1926
Treasure of the Sierra Nevada, The	2009
Tremors	1990
Trial and Error	1997
Tycoon	1947
Under Mexicali Stars	1950
Under Western Stars	1938
Unexpected Guest	1947
Untamed Breed, The	1948
Utah	1945
Valley of Fire	1951
Violent Men, The	1955
Violent Ones, The	1967
Violent Road	1958
Virginian, The	1923
Viva Cisco Kid	1940
Wagon Master, The	1929
Wagons Westward	1940
Walking Hills, The	1949
Wanderer of the Wasteland	1935
Wanderer of the Wasteland	1945
War Party	1965
Water Rustlers	1939
Water, Water Everywhere	1920
Waterhole #3	1967
West of Nevada	1936
West of the Pecos	1945
Western Frontier	1935
Western Gold	1937
Western Heritage	1948
Western Rover, The	1927
Westward Ho	1935
What I Did For Love	2006
Wheels of Destiny	1934
Where the Buffalo Roam	1938
Whistling Jim	1925
White Outlaw, The	1925
White Thunder	1925
Wide Open Town	1941
Wild Bill: Hollywood Maverick	1995
Wild Horse Mesa	1947
Wild Horse Rodeo	1937
Wild Horse Stampede, The	1926
Wild Westerners, The	1962
Winning of the West	1953
Woman Hungry	1931
Woman Trap	1936
Yellow Sky	1948
Zabriskie Point	1970

continued from page 93

here as TV's "Wild Bill Hickok" by fishing in Lone Pine Creek. He also told of *Gunga Din* days when he was one of those hundreds of Thuggee bad guys getting shot off their horses in the long shots, wrapped head to toe in those white bed-sheets. "I know you recognized me," he joked.

Richard Martin (Chito to both Robert Mitchum and Tim Holt) said they used to pray that none of the RKO executives ever came up because "if they ever saw how much fun we had here in Lone Pine, they wouldn't pay us ANY-thing and we got precious little as it was!"

And Montie Montana, another faithful Lone Pine supporter, recalled doubling William Boyd once (that shot in *Law of the Pampas* when Hoppy leans down out of the saddle at a gallop to scoop up that bolo). He also remembered Boyd telling everyone that whenever any of the Lone Pine kids came out to the set, "Don't you ever turn them away. Make sure they stay for lunch and have a good seat to watch us work." (Lots of locals remember that, too - Dr. Don Christenson remembers being one of those kids getting a pat on the shoulder out there from Hoppy. And they all remember similar standing orders on the Gene Autry and Roy Rogers sets, too.)

Once when director William Witney was asked, "Of all the cowboy stars you worked with, who was the best horseman?" he answered without hesitation, "Roy Rogers," prompting George Montgomery to say, "And he was, too." But he had to add with a grin, as he drew himself up to his full six-feet-two, "among the shorter fellas."

The year we celebrated the 50th anniversary of Robert Mitchum's first starring role (in a picture done here, 1944's *Nevada*), a film commitment prevented his attending so he graciously sat still for a special 20-minute video interview we showed that weekend. In it, he chatted with Charles Champlin[22] and told such stories as how, when they'd be roasting (shooting) in what he called the "alkali flats" east of Lone Pine,[23] the wranglers would gallop by the camera, "accidentally" spattering dust in it so everyone could collapse in the shade of the trucks while things got cleaned up.

the museum and special events

Of course, as of 2005 you don't have to wait til October to get your fill of movie memories here. Now you can inspect the past any time you visit Lone Pine. At the 2005 Film Festival, everyone celebrated the long-awaited opening of The Lone Pine Film History Museum (formerly The Beverly and Jim Rogers Museum of Lone Pine Film History). Among its possessions is the original Twentieth Century Fox stagecoach they used here in 1951's *Rawhide*.

To help acquire the museum land (just south of the high school), special summer fundraising events were held for years. Among the most memorable was 1993's celebration of the 60th anniversary of The Lone Ranger and 1995's Hopalong Cassidy Centennial, the weekend Mr. Boyd would have been a 100.

A highlight of the Ranger weekend was James King conducting a 28-piece symphony orchestra out in the rocks one night at the Lone Ranger ambush site and playing Lone Ranger excerpts from Les Preludes, the William Tell Overture and Republic's 1938 serial score.

And people say that something they'll never forget from the Hoppy weekend was seeing the very first Hopalong Cassidy movie out under-the-stars one night in a deep canyon close to where they actually filmed some of it 60 years before. We watched the fight at the hideout cabin at the end and walked right by the same spot on our way back to the busses.

For several years each June, we gather a group of 300 or so in the hills for the dinner and Concert in the Rocks. Dine as the sun sets. Watch the lights rise illuminating the surrounding rocks. Enjoy music under the stars.

If you aren't on our mailing list, write Box 111, Lone Pine CA 93545 or visit the website www.lonepinefilmhistorymuseum.org and you'll be kept posted on what's going on.

Getting the picture? The fun never stops. Neither does the filming. Hollywood is still coming up here.

tv, too

You saw basketball great Michael Jordan in that commerical directed by Ridley Scott, who has done several spots up here between features (remember his Jeep driver asking directions over the mountains?). And Willie Nelson and Waylon Jennings were here selling pizza. And Jack Palance returned to Lone Pine to herd cows in tha pickup (he did *The Lonely Man* and *I Died A Thousand Times* here, remember). Even "Crocodile Dundee," Paul Hogan, out-smarted some bad guys here in a 4-wheel drive vehicle.

But it isn't only in commercials that you see Lone Pine on TV. For the hit *Star Trek Voyager* series, Kate Mulgrew and her crew were up here, only to be stranded on some bizarre planet at the end of the spring '96 season. It was a two-parter so when the

---

18 Coordinated by Riverwood Press's Packy Smith, the B-Western historian who started all this movie convention business 42 years ago. With two friends, he put on the very first Western Film Festival in 1972 in Memphis, Tennessee
19 By private auto or passenger busses, live guides tell you what happened down that canyon and over there.
20 Might be arranged through the McGee Creek Pack Station.
21 Big plaques, little plaques, they're everywhere. Lone Pine is proud of its movie history. The Best Western Frontier even has deluxe rooms named after stars who worked here or stayed at the motel over the years. The Gregory Peck room, the Roy Rogers room . .
22 Arts Editor Emeritus of the L.A. Times
23 Working on West of the Pecos (1945).
24 Just West of Movie Road on Whitney Portal Road, so-called because the movie town of "Red Dog" was built nearby for a Technicolor musical Western, Song of the West (1930). The set stood abandoned for so long, it gave its name to the area.
25 Studios shot up here so much. they accumulated tons of shots of scenery or generic bad guys shooting up the ranch or racing through the rocks or whatever and would often use those shots behind a film's credits or to pad out montages. But just having stock footage in a film doesn't qualify that film for the list. The footage has to have been shot specifically for that picture, not taken from the library.
26 At The Indian Trading Post, where Errol Flynn, Gary Cooper et al did the very same when they were here!

fall season began, they were still out in the Alabama Hills (last seen just north of the *Rawhide* burial site). And I never did know what the commercial was for, but back in '91, Dudley Moore was out in the Alabams for something that maybe just aired back East. Do you know? Write us.

you can help

Also write if you know of a Lone Pine picture that isn't on this new combined list. Because our work certainly isn't done. That's why when we mention the titles we've accumulated, we add "so far." The list is not complete yet. We're forever following leads. And sometimes, sorting it all out gets complicated.

Long-time Lone Pine residents remember when the silent screen's "It" Girl, Clara Bow, was here visiting hubby Rex Bell. He was starring in a Western but she was just visiting, not working they say. But which picture was it? What name do we add to the list? The new additions include a Rex Bell western from 1936 but it's thought the Bow visit was earlier than that.

Since Bow and Bell didn't meet and marry until 1931, it couldn't have been one of the four Westerns he made for Fox in 1928. So we don't have to find and look at those to see if any were done here. But what about that string of nine he did for Monogram in 1932 and 1933 (he didn't do any Westerns in between)? Was it one of those? Or one of another nine he did for Resolute and Colony in '35 and '36 (not counting the ones we've verified)?

An added fillip: Chris Langley reminds us that "people used to call the bridge at Red Dog "Bow Bridge"[24] because Clara Bow ran her car off it once." (During that same visit, probably?) So it'll be a well-rounded story once we close in on the correct title(s) - if we haven't already.

The point is, you be one of those who calls or writes to say, "Check out this story" or "I just watched such-and-such and it opens in Lone Pine!" Please don't ever assume we must know about that one since the star's so big and the rocks so obvious. Tell us anyway, like the fans who write to say that Lone Pine is in the "Superman" and "Captain Marvel" serials. It is but it's stock footage[25] (the latter from *Storm Over Bengal*). But often, someone mentions a title we don't have. And it gets checked and maybe added.

Stuntman Neil Summers is forever sending stills and lobby cards for the archives, sometimes of "new" titles, certainly of new views so we can pin-point new filming sites.

And you always run into Lone Pine mentions in Hollywood biographies.

And Leonard Maltin calls about hundreds of stills from silent films that he bought at an estate sale. "I'm sure there are Lone Pine locations in them," he said. "Come look!"

And someone else calls with a title they saw on Encore's Western channel. And others send along photos they've found. And stories. And questions.

And so . . . the search still goes on.

Historic Marker at the corner of Whitney Portal Road and Movie Road
(GPS Extra 5)

the lone pine quiz
what was buster keaton doing here?

This list serves a triple purpose.

Not only does it alphabetize in one spot *most* of the "names" who have worked in and around Lone Pine — a few of which might be obscure to all but the most devoted film and serial buff — but it also serves as a fast reference to who was here, what they were in (or what they did) and in some cases, other roles you might associate with them.

Thirdly, it's a dandy quiz to give yourself or that guy who knows it all (who knows? Maybe he does; this is one way to find out.) And if you're in a crowd with *two* know-it-alls, watch them begin competing with each other and give you more answers than you want on some of these. (Unsolicited, they'll tell you the year of the films, the studio, the director, who else was in it, other things so-and-so did, etc.)

Sometimes, the descriptions are overly simple; i.e., rather than list all the films certain people worked on here, you'll find Henry Hathaway listed simply as "Director," Gabby Hayes as "Hoppy sidekick (Roy's, too)" and just "Several films here" for people like Autry, Rogers and Wayne.

Behind many of the "answers" are numbers in parentheses. If you're using this as a quiz, these will tell you how many answers (how many points) to look for in that particular description. (Where no numbers are listed, the number is obvious.)

Looking at it from the quiz-giver's standpoint, the number indicates how many questions you can find among the material at hand. To give you specific examples, the questions are given where necessary in the first 20. Those will give you the idea; from then on, the questions hopefully will be self-evident.

Not on this list, by the way, are many of your favorite screen villains (Roy Barcroft, Harry Woods, Harry Lauter, Bud Osborne, Anthony Caruso, Ray Teal, Robert Kortman, Dick Curtis, Jack Ingram, Kenne Duncan, George Chesebro, I. Stanford Jolley, Tom London, John Merton, etc.) They're missing only for the sake of brevity; suffice it to say that all of them — *all* of them — worked out in those rocks, too.

So here we go...

Jack Hoxie.

WHO ARE THEY AND WHAT WERE THEY DOING HERE?

1. Eddie Acuff
2. John Agar
3. Claude Akins
4. Kay Aldridge
5. Rex Allen
6. Warner Anderson
7. Morris Ankrum
8. Fatty Arbuckle
9. George Archainbaud
10. Gene Autry
11. Robert Barratt
12. Don 'Red' Barry
13. Kevin Bacon
14. Anne Baxter
15. Noah Beery Jr.
16. Wallace Beery

THE QUIZ CONTINUES

17. Bruce Bennett
18. Spencer Gordon Bennett
19. James Best
20. Amanda Blake
21. Dan Blocker
22. Humphrey Bogart
23. John Boles
24. Ward Bond
25. Richard Boone
26. Ernest Borgnine
27. Walter Brennan
28. Steve Brodie
29. Rand Brooks
30. Joe E. Brown
31. Johnny Mack Brown
32. Smiley Burnette
33. Pat Buttram
34. William Boyd
35. Rod Cameron
36. Yakima Canutt
37. John Carradine
38. Cass County Boys
39. Lane Chandler
40. Lon Chaney, Jr.
41. Andy Clyde
42. Edmund S. Cobb
43. James Coburn
44. Bill Cody
45. Iron Eyes Cody
46. Tris Coffin
47. Gary Cooper
48. Robert Coote
49. Ray Corrigan
50. Bing Crosby
51. Tony Curtis
52. Linda Darnell
53. Gail Davis
54. Laraine Day
55. Eddie Dean
56. John Derek
57. Andy Devine
58. John Doucette
59. James Drury
60. Robert Duvall
61. Brian Donlevy
62. Jeff Donnell
63. Kirk Douglas
64. Clint Eastwood
65. Blake Edwards
66. Jack Elam
67. William Elliott
68. James Ellison
69. John English
70. Dale Evans
71. Douglas Fairbanks Jr.
72. Peter Falk
73. Richard Farnsworth
74. Frank Faylen
75. Paul Fix
76. Jay C. Flippen
77. Errol Flynn
78. Henry Fonda
79. Glenn Ford
80. Joan Fontaine
81. Preston Foster
82. Douglas Fowley
83. James Garner
84. Hoot Gibson
85. Frances Gifford
86. James Gleason
87. Cary Grant
88. Lorne Green
89. Michael Gross
90. Alan Hale Jr.
91. Barbara Hale
92. Thurston Hall
93. Stuart Hamblen
94. John Hart
95. Henry Hathaway
96. Russell Hayden
97. George 'Gabby' Hayes
98. Susan Hayward
99. Rita Hayworth
100. Jack Holt
101. Tim Holt
102. Jack Hoxie
103. Sam Jaffe
104. Anne Jeffreys
105. Buck Jones
106. Dick Jones
107. Victor Jory
108. Joe Kane
109. Buster Keaton
110. Brian Keith
111. Paul Kelly
112. Arthur Kennedy
113. Brad King
114. Henry King
115. Jay Kirby
116. Patric Knowles
117. Martin Landau
118. Michael Landon
119. Allan Lane
120. Richard Lane
121. Robert Lansing
122. Jack Lemmon
123. Robert Livingstone
124. Frank Lovejoy
125. Ida Lupino
126. Cliff Lyons
127. Guy Madison
128. Jock Mahoney
129. Karl Malden
130. Hugh Marlowe
131. Richard Martin
132. Lee Marvin
133. Ken Maynard
134. Virginia Mayo
135. Francis McDonald
136. Frank McGlynn Jr.
137. Victor McLaglen
138. Steve McQueen
139. Martin Milner
140. Robert Mitchum
141. Tom Mix
142. George Montgomery
143. Clayton Moore
144. Terry Moore
145. Harry Morgan
146. Chester Morris
147. Audie Murphy
148. Don Murray
149. David Niven
150. Edmond O'Brien
151. Pat O'Brien
152. Maureen O'Hara
153. Maureen O"Sullivan
154. Jack Palance
155. Gregory Peck
156. George Peppard
157. Anthony Perkins
158. Paul Picerni
159. Slim Pickens
160. Lee Powell
161. Tyrone Power
162. Robert Preston
163. Anthony Quinn
164. Vera Hruba Ralston
165. Jack Randall
166. George Reeves
167. Duncan Renaldo
168. Michael Rennie
169. Kane Richmond
170. Pernell Roberts
171. Edward G. Robinson
172. Jimmy Rogers
173. Cesar Romero
174. Roy Rogers
175. Will Rogers?
176. Robert Ryan
177. Sheila Ryan
178. John Russell
179. Randolph Scott
180. Al St. John
181. Lesley Selander
182. Joseph Schildkraut
183. Johnny Sheffield
184. Reginald Sheffield
185. Harry Sherman
186. Jay Silverheels
187. Sons of the Pioneers
188. Barbara Stanwyck
189. George Stevens
190. Elaine Stewart
191. Peggy Stewart
192. Dean Stockwell
193. Glenn Strange
194. Hal Taliaferro
195. William Tallman
196. Forrest Taylor
197. Max Terhune
198. Chief Thundercloud
199. George Tobias
200. Sidney Toler
201. Franchot Tone
202. John Travolta
203. Sonny Tufts
204. Tom Tyler
205. John Wayne
206. Michael Wayne
207. Patrick Wayne
208. Johnny Weismuller
209. William Wellman
210. Stuart Whitman
211. Richard Widmark
212. Bill Williams
213. Guinn 'Big Boy' Williams
214. Shelley Winters
215. Grant Withers
216. William Witney
217. Britt Wood
218. NatalieWood
219. Keenan Wynn
220. Joe Yrigoyen

Answers begin on page 102

Steve McQueen as *Nevada Smith* (1966).

The Olivas brothers always swore Wallace Beery made a picture in Lone Pine but no-one remembered what until this photo turned up in the Academy of Motion Picture Arts and Sciences files. He not only worked here but it was in the area's first film, *The Roundup* with Fatty Arbuckle. That's the young slim Beery in the center. Other foreground players are (from left) Arbuckle, Eddie Sutherland, Tom Forman and Jeanne Acker.

Courtesy of the Academy of Motion Picture Arts and Sciences.

A GROUP SHOT with the cast and crew of the Hopalong Cassidy Western, *Range War* (1939), taken at the new hacienda/mission set on Russ Spainhower's Anchor Ranch. This quite probably was the first movie to have used the new set, which might well be the reason for such a commemorative group shot. In the center of the front row is William Boyd (Hoppy). To his right (wearing Hoppy's hat) is producer Harry Sherman. Next to him is the director, Lesley Selander. At the left end of the front row is Eddie Dean, later a cowboy singing star in his own right. To Boyd's left are Russell Hayden and Britt Wood. Also look for Montie Montana and the doubles for Hoppy and Lucky.

the answers

1. Jack's sidekick in *Jungle Girl* was Allan Lane's sidekick here in *Daredevils of the West*. (4 — In what serial did he appear here? *Daredevils of the West*. In what role? Allan Lane's sidekick. In what other famous serial (not done here) did he appear? *Jungle Girl*. In what role? Jack's sidekick.)
2. *Along the Great Divide*.
3. TV's "Sheriff Lobo" and today's radio voice for Aamco Transmissions was here with Randolph Scott in *Comanche Station*. (4 — In what picture did he work here? *Comanche Station*. Who starred in that? Randolph Scott. What was his popular TV role? Sheriff Lobo. Why is his voice so familiar? Radio spokesman for...etc.)
4. Republic's second "Nyoka" (in *The Perils of Nyoka*) was the female lead here in *Daredevils of the West*. (4 — In what serial did she appear here? *Daredevils of the West*. In what capacity? The female lead. In what other serial (not done here) did she star? *The Perils of Nyoka*. What was significant about that role? She was the second actress to play "Nyoka" for Republic.)
5. *Under Mexicali Stars*.
6. *Violent Men*.
7. Hoppy villain.
8. Starred in first film here, *The Roundup*. (2 — In what film did he appear here? *The Roundup*. What was significant about that film? It was the first film shot here.)
9. Director.
10. Several films here.
11. Cisco Kid film.
12. Republic's "Red Ryder" was here on *Plainsman and the Lady*, also as Roy's brother in *Saga Of Death Valley*. (4 — In what two films did he appear here? *Plainsman and the Lady* and *Saga Of Death Valley*. What role did he play in the latter? Roy Rogers's brother. For what role is he the most famous? The serial "Red Ryder.")
13. *Tremors*.
14. *Yellow Sky*.
15. Indian chief in Tim Holt's *Indian Agent*. (3 — In what picture did he work here? *Indian Agent*. In what role? Indian chief. Who starred in that picture? Tim Holt.)
16. In first film here, *The Roundup*. (Same as 8 above.)
17. *Lone Ranger* serial.
18. Director.
19. Randolph Scott Western.
20. TV's Miss Kitty ("Gunsmoke") here on *Adventures of Hajii Baba*. (2 — In what film did she appear here? *Adventures etc*. For what role is she best remembered? Miss Kitty on "Gunsmoke.") Got the idea now?
21. Here on a "Bonanza."
22. *High Sierra*.
23. *Song of the West*.
24. Later the wagon boss on TV's *Wagon Train*, he was a bad guy in Ken Maynard's *Cattle Thief*. (5)
25. TV's *Have Gun, Will Travel* and with Randolph Scott in *The Tall T*. (3)
26. *Bad Day At Black Rock*.
27. *Along the Great Divide*, *Bad Day At Black Rock*. (2)
28. Tim Holt villain.
29. Scarlett's first husband was "Lucky" in the last dozen Hoppy features, four of which were done here. (4)
30. Here in *Song of the West*.
31. *Between Men* and *Born To The West* (the latter with Wayne).
32. Gene Autry sidekick.
33. Gene Autry sidekick.
34. Hoppy himself.
35. *Brimstone*.
36. Stunt man.
37. Bob Ford in 1939's *Jesse James* worked with Power again in *Brigham Young* here. (3)
38. Autry's *Trail To San Antone*.
39. *Lone Ranger* serial.
40. The "Wolfman" himself was here on *Springfield Rifle*. (2)
41. Hoppy's sidekick, "California." (2)
42. The Ranger captain in *Lone Ranger* serial. (2)
43. *Waterhole No. 3*.
44. *Frontier Days*.
45. Tim Holt Western.
46. The Lone Ranger's brother on TV was here on Autry's *Trail To San Antone*. (3)
47. *Lives of A Bengal Lancer* and *Springfield Rifle*. (2)
48. Here as Ballantine's replacement, Sgt. Higginbotham, in *Gunga Din*, Coote was also seen over the years as head of the Binet players in *Scaramouche*, one of the *Three Musketeers* in the 1948 Gene Kelly version and as the bogus Charles Stuart touring the Netherlands in Doug Jr.'s wonderful *The Exile*. (9)
49. Three Mesquiteers Western (*Gunsmoke Ranch*.) (2)
50. *Rhythm on the Range*.
51. *The Great Race*.
52. *Brigham Young*.
53. Gene Autry film and also here as TV's "Annie Oakley." (2)
54. *Tycoon*.
55. Hoppy Western.
56. *Adventures of Hajii Baba*.
57. With TV's "Wild Bill Hickok."
58. "The Dude" on a "Lone Ranger" TV episode was here on *Nevada Smith*. (2)
59. Randolph Scott Western.
60. "Lonesome Dove" co-star here on *Joe Kidd*. (2)
61. *Brigham Young*.
62. Tim Holt's *Stagecoach Kid*. (2)
63. *Along the Great Divide*. It was his first Western role. (2)
64. *Joe Kidd*.
65. Directed *Great Race*.
66. *Rawhide*.
67. *Plainsman and the Lady*.
68. Hoppy sidekick.
69. Director.
70. Mrs. Rogers.
71. *Gunga Din*.
72. TV's "Colombo" was here on *The Great Race*. (2)
73. Early day stunts here.
74. Randolph Scott Western.
75. John Wayne films.
76. *From Hell To Texas*.
77. *Charge of the Light Brigade* and *Kim*. (2)
78. *How The West Was Won*.
79. *Violent Men* and *The Loves of Carmen*. (2)
80. *Gunga Din*.
81. *Army Girl*.
82. Hoppy villain.
83. Here for a *Rockford Files* TV episode.
84. Universal Westerns.
85. Republic's first "Nyoka" (in *Jungle Girl*) was here in Hoppy's *Border Vigilantes*. (4)
86. *Tycoon*.
87. *Gunga Din*.
88. Here on "Bonanza."

Tom Mix in *Terror Trail* (1933).

89. Alex's dad on TV's "Family Ties" here on *Tremors*. (3)
90. The Captain on TV's "Gilligan's Island" wanted to kill *The Gunfighter* here. (3)
91. TV's Della Street was here with Mitchum in *West of the Pecos*. (3)
92. Walter Mitty's boss was here in *West of The Pecos*. (2)
93. *Plainsman and the Lady*.
94. Here first as *Jack Armstrong*, then as a TV *Lone Ranger*. (2)
95. Director.
96. Hoppy sidekick.
97. Hoppy sidekick (Roy's, too). (2)
98. *Rawhide*.
99. *Loves of Carmen*.
100. With son Tim in *Arizona Rangers*. (2)
101. Several films here.
102. Universal Westerns.
103. "Gunga Din" himself.
104. The screen's first Tess Trueheart (to Morgan Conway's *Dick Tracy* (1945)) and one of the Kirbys on TV's *Topper*, she was Mitchum's leading lady here in his first starring film, *Nevada*.
105. Several pix, inc. *Roaring West*.
106. TV's Buffalo Bill Jr.
107. Frequent Hoppy villain.
108. Director.
109. Unbilled extra in *The Roundup* as a favor to his friend, Arbuckle.
110. *Violent Men* and *Nevada Smith*. (2)
111. *Springfield Rifle*.
112. *Nevada Smith*.
113. Hoppy sidekick.
114. Director.
115. Hoppy sidekick.
116. *Charge of the Light Brigade*.
117. *Nevada Smith*.
118. TV's "Bonanza."
119. The voice of TV's "Mr. Ed" starred here in *Daredevils of the West*. (3)
120. Lt. Farraday to Chester Morris's "Boston Blackie" was here on Montgomery's *Riders of the Purple Sage*. (4)
121. *Eye for an Eye*.
122. *The Great Race*.
123. The screen's second Lone Ranger was one of the Three Mesquiteers here in *Gunsmoke Ranch*. (3)
124. *The Hitchhiker*.
125. *High Sierra* and back to direct *The Hitchhiker*. (3)
126. Stunt man.
127. TV's "Wild Bill Hickok."
128. Gene Autry Western.
129. *Nevada Smith*.
130. *Rawhide*.
131. Tim Holt's Chito. (2)
132. Randolph Scott Western and *I Died A Thousand Times*. (2)
133. Several films here, sound *and* silent.
134. *Along the Great Divide*.
135. Hoppy villain.
136. John Wayne's brother in *Westward Ho*, Red Connors in *Bar 20 Rides Again*. (4)
137. *Gunga Din*.
138. *Nevada Smith*.
139. TV's *Route 66* and *Adam 12* star was here in *Springfield Rifle*. (3)
140. Six pictures here: the lead in *Nevada* and *West of the Pecos* and both bad guy and good guy in four Hopalong Cassidy Westerns. (He was in seven Hoppys all-together.) (6)
141. Parts of two silents and two sound films here. (2)
142. *Lone Ranger* serial and *Riders of the Purple Sage*. (2)
143. *Lone Ranger* (TV).
144. *King of the Khyber Rifles*.
145. Sgt. Friday's last *Dragnet* partner and the head doc on *M*A*S*H* was one of the bank robbers in *Yellow Sky*. (7)
146. "Boston Blackie" in all those Columbia detective pictures was here in *Wagons Westward*. (2)
147. Our most decorated soldier in WWII was here for *Hell Bent For Texas* and others.
148. *From Hell To Texas*.
149. *Charge of the Light Brigade*.
150. *The Hitchhiker*.
151. *Oil For The Lamps of China*.
152. *Bagdad*.
153. Tarzan's best Jane was here in *The Tall T* (Randolph Scott). (3)
154. *The Lonely Man* and *I Died A Thousand Times*. (2)
155. Three films here.
156. The head of TV's "A Team" was here in *How The West Was Won*. (2)
157. *Psycho*'s Norman Bates was here in *The Lonely Man*. (3)
158. One of TV's "Untouchables" was here in *Adventures of Hajii Baba*. (2)
159. *Eye For An Eye*.
160. Was the Lone Ranger in the first serial.
161. Three films here.
162. *How The West Was Won*.
163. *Tycoon*.
164. The wife of the head of Republic was here in *Plainsman and the Lady*. (2)
165. Bob Livingston's older brother was here in *Riders of the Dawn*. (2)
166. TV's "Superman" was a Hoppy sidekick. (2)
167. TV's "Cisco Kid" was here with both Hoppy and Roy. (3)
168. *King of the Khyber Rifles*.
169. Republic's "Spy Smasher" here in *Jungle Raiders* serial. (2)
170. With "Bonanza."
171. Even "Little Caesar" was here (in *Violent Men*.) (2)
172. Hoppy sidekick.
173. The Joker on TV's "Batman" did four *Cisco Kid* pictures here. (3)
174. Several films here.
175. Possibly *Water, Water Everywhere*.
176. *Bad Day At Black Rock*.
177. Mrs. Pat Buttram here in Roy's *Song of Texas* and as a crooked female sheriff with hubby and Gene in *Mule Train*. (6)
178. TV's "Lawman" a bad man in *Yellow Sky*. (2)
179. Several films here.
180. "Fuzzy" to Buster Crabbe and Lash LaRue was here as a Hoppy crook. (4)
181. Director.
182. *Plainsman and the Lady*.
183. *Tarzan's Desert Mystery*.
184. Johnny Sheffield's father was Kipling in *Gunga Din*. (3)

185. Long-time Hoppy producer.
186. TV's Tonto to both Moore and Hart here. (3)
187. Roy Rogers Westerns.
188. *Violent Men.*
189. Director.
190. *Adventures Of Hajii Baba.*
191. Gene Autry Western.
192. The "Boy with Green Hair" here as *Kim*. (2)
193. Several films here as good guys *and* bad guys.
194. *Lone Ranger* serial.
195. Prosecutor Ham Burger on TV's "Perry Mason" was here on *The Hitchhiker*. (3)
196. *Jungle Raiders.*
197. "Lullaby" here in that Three Mesquiteers Western, then returned for *Rawhide*. (3)
198. Tonto in the *Lone Ranger* serials. (2)
199. *Rawhide.*
200. "Charlie Chan" here with Hoppy in *Law of the Pampas*. (2)
201. *Lives Of A Bengal Lancer.*
202. *Perfect.*
203. *Untamed Breed.*
204. Hoppy villain (*Border Vigilantes*). (2)
205. Several films here (including last appearance on film in that Great Western Savings commercial.) (2)
206. The Wayne son who now runs Batjac Productions was here as a second assistant director on Batjac's *Seven Men From Now* in 1956. (4)
207. Another Wayne son; *Eye For An Eye*.
208. *Tarzan's Desert Mystery.*
209. Director.
210. TV's "Cimarron Strip."
211. *Yellow Sky* and *Law and Jake Wade*.
212. TV's "Kit Carson" here with wife-to-be Barbara Hale in *West of the Pecos*. (4)
213. *Springfield Rifle* and *Nevada*. (2)
214. *I Died A Thousand Times.*
215. *Tycoon* and *Utah*. (2)
216. Director.
217. Hoppy sidekick.
218. *The Great Race.*
219. *The Great Race.*
220. Stunt double for Autry and Rogers.

Clockwise: George Peppard (with Mt. Whitney above) in *How The West Was Won*, Randolph Scott in *Comanche Station* (there was often enough water in aqueduct spillways to make movie rivers) and Kirk Douglas (right) in his first Western, *Along the Great Divide*.

DAVE HOLLAND is the author of two previous books, *The Secret of the Old Church* (a children's mystery) and the 444-page *From Out of the Past: A Pictorial History of the Lone Ranger*, both available from the Holland House in Granada Hills, California. He was a former newspaperman, theatrical press agent, advertising and p.r. director and film production manager and assistant director. Co-founder and Director of the Lone Pine Film Festival for its first decade, he also produced two DVDs on movie locations, "*On Location In Lone Pine*" 1 and 2.

the author's acknowledgments

AS WRITTEN FOR THE 1990 EDITION

So many helped make this book a reality....sharing rare photographs from private collections and scrapbooks, sharing personal experiences from the Movie Days, flying me over those spectacular rocks so I could get aerial photos for the map drawings.

There were so many long conversations into the night (talking about Lone Pine movies), long hours with the VCR (watching, studying those movies), long hot hikes through the Alabama Hills (searching for where they shot those movies) — I've been doing these things for years with people who shared my love of Lone Pine and what happened here.

The *individual* things people did to help are too numerous to mention — but not the people who did 'em, so at last, let me publicly thank:

Rellis Amick, Joy Anderson, Ken Baxter, Dorothy Bonnefin, Rand Brooks, Ada Brown, Harold 'Swede' and Robbye Carrasco, Manuel Castro, Delia Cederburg, Roy Cline, Irene Cuffe, Carolyn Curtis, Mario DeMarco, Andrew Escalona, Marty Forstenzer, John Hart, Curt Herring, Holly Holland, Mike Holland, Dick Iacobellis, Larry Imber, Loren Janes, Carol Jobim, Mike Johnson, Jim Johnstone, Richard and Diane Kennedy, Birgitte Kueppers, Andy Marsh, Ann-Marie McCollum, Dick Miller, Jim Mitchell, Nancy Monkman, Clayton Moore, Mark and Melody Ogburn, Ethel Olivas, Pete Olivas, Polly Parker, Francis Pedneau, Rod Philbrook, David Rothel, Mike Royer, Abdol-Hossain Sharif, Bill and Norma Shelton, Bob Sherman, Peggy Shervais, Dr. George and Hazel Shultz, Mary Sinclair, Dave Smirnoff, Packy Smith, Steve and Gail Stewart, Brent Taylor, Ken Taylor, Jack Wilson, William Witney, Bob Wolter, K.C. Wylie and Joe Yrigoyen.

Included in that group are those who ventured out into the rocks with me when they could, the brave souls who quickly learned to feel like U.S. mail carriers because neither rain nor snow nor wind nor blistering heat (and we hit 'em all) kept us from our task: spending hours matching photographs to the distant mountains, lining them up with foreground formations to pinpoint specific locations, to find *exactly* where a certain *Gunga Din* battle was staged, where Natalie Wood became a world-class tire-kicker in *The Great Race* or where Tyrone Power was tied to that stake in *King of the Khyber Rifles*.

Deserving of special thanks are Lynne Bunn and Jeanne Willey of the Dow Villa (and Yolanda and Rosalie and all the rest) for their kindnesses over the years, Bill Michaels and Kathy Barnes of the Eastern California Museum, Nancy Tallent of the Inyo County Council of the Arts, Jodi Stewart and Mike Patterson up in Cerro Gordo, Bob Sherman of Iverson's Movie Location Ranch, Susan Oka and her staff at the Academy of Motion Picture Arts and Sciences, Robin Bolger of the George Eastman House and Raymond Powell, president of the Lone Pine Chamber of Commerce. Many thanks to them for their generous support — and to Kerry Powell, who coordinated Lone Pine's first annual Sierra Film Festival in October, 1990. What fun it was working on that. I thank her for the opportunity to help.

Certain reference works are mentioned either in the text or footnotes (like Rudy Behlmer's *AMERICA'S FAVORITE MOVIES I Behind The Scenes*). I urge you to track them all down and add them to your library.

MUSIC IN THE BACKGROUND

There's always been music in the background where the Alabama Hills were concerned. First there were groups like this one to set the mood while filming the silent movies, now you can pop in a cassette while you're slowly driving those dirt roads. But keep it appropriate. Make it music from Republic westerns or music you heard in the Lone Ranger serial.

more to read, more to see

To bring this history even more alive, add Dave's two DVDs to your collection. Watch Dave discuss a movie at the same spot where they shot the original. Then he fades from view and the scene in the movie fills the screen. You'll see the rocks and area have hardly changed at all! The first DVD focuses on the locations in and around Lone Pine. The second encompasses locations from as far north as Mono County and as far south as Los Angeles County. Each one is almost 2 hours long, taking you to a few spots you've never seen and telling you some stories you've never heard. We support the locals in Lone Pine so please purchase through the many stores in town or via their websites as well as the museum's (real or online) gift shop. We thank you very much!

A lot of the films shot on location in Lone Pine (*Gunga Din, Rawhide, How The West Was Won*, etc.) are available at the splendid Gift Shop in the Lone Pine museum. They have a comprehensive selection of items in their online store as well. From belt buckles, CDs, posters, t-shirts, to antiques and film festival memorabilia, you'll find treasures to keep and to share, educate and entertain! For more information on the movies and the area visit:

Lone Pine Film History Museum
701 S. Main Street
Lone Pine, CA 93545
760-876-9909
Visit www.lonepinefilmhistorymuseum.org
Write to them at: P. O. Box 111
Lone Pine, CA 93545

AND one mile south of Lone Pine:
Eastern Sierra Interagency Visitor Center
US Hwy. 395 and SR 136
Lone Pine, CA 93545
760-876-6222

Wondering more about Roy Rogers? Contact his daughter and supporter of all things Lone Pine, Cheryl Rogers Barnett. She loves to share stories and has several books published about her mom and dad.
Her website is www.cherylrogers.com

Some of the Gene Autry Lone Pine films are available at:
Autry National Center
4700 Western Heritage Drive
Los Angeles, CA 90027
323-667-2000 or
www.theautry.org
Also, contact the following for rental and sales information on some 60,000 titles, including the "B" westerns and serials:

Eddie Brandt's Saturday Matinee
5006 Vineland Ave.
North Hollywood, CA 91601
818-506-4242
www.ebsmvideo.com
Yep, the store is still there!

And if this book whets your movie location appetite, the author, David Rothel, will treat you in any of his thirteen books on various aspects of show business. His "An Ambush of Ghosts: A Guide to Favorite Western Film Locations" covers, just as the title suggests, several filming sites (including Monument Valley, Old Tucson and many more). Many Rothel books are available at the museum!

Boyd Magers' book "Gene Autry Westerns" is still available in print but there's his location book you'll want to read. More sites are detailed in "So You Wanna See Cowboy Stuff? The Western Movie-TV Tour Guide" and includes research by locations expert Tinsley Yarbrough.

You'll want to read Robert G. Sherman's 1984 book "Quiet on The Set" detailing the movie history at Iverson Movie Ranch in Chatsworth, CA

With the Internet access, there's a plethora blogs of the film sites. Yet, so many books various locations in the West are perhaps st available at:

Larry Edmunds Bookshop
6644 Hollywood Blvd.
Los Angeles, CA 90028
323-463-3273
Visit www.larryedmunds.com
And, yes, this store is still there, too!

New this year is Charles Michael Morfin's "Location Filming in the Alabama Hills" published by Arcadia Publishing in their Images of America series. Captured in unique pictorial format, the book has a couple hundred images celebrating the area movie making history. Find it at the Lone Pine Film History Museum Gift Shop or through www.arcadiapublishing.com.

As for the many locations Republic Pictures used, there's a section on that in *Republic – The Studio*. Jack Mathis' wonderful collection is at Brigham Young University in Provo, Utah, www.byu.edu.

GPS Coordinates Chart

Page # in Book	Location # in Book	GPS Latitude/Longitue Decimal Degrees		Latitude/Longitude Degrees Minutes/Seconds		Latitude/Longitude Degrees Decimal Minutes		UTM Easting/Northing	
30	1	N 36.61029*	W 118.12779*	N 36* 36' 37.2"	W 118* 7' 40.0"	N 36* 36.617	W 118* 7.66777	399142	4052235
30	2	N 36.609637*	W 118.12487*	N 36*36' 34.694"	W 118* 7' 29.5"	N 36* 36.578	W 118* 7.492	399402	4052158
30	3	N 36.610515*	W 118.118187*	N 36* 36' 37.856"	W 118* 7' 5.474"	N36* 36.63093	W 118* 7.091233	400001	4052248
30	4	N 36.60829*	W 118.12684*	N 36* 36' 29.9"	W 118* 7' 36.6"	N 36* 36.5000'	W 118* 7.610	399225	4052011
30	5	N 36.6037806*	W 118.1188202*	N 36* 36' 13.61"	W 118* 7' 7.753"	N 36* 36.231	W 118* 07.122	399935	4051502
30	6	N 36.6039446*	W 118.1169746*	N 36* 36' 14.201"	W 118* 7' 1.109"	N 36* 36.236	W 118* 7.018483	400101	4051518
30	7	N 36.5984298*	W 118.1165154*	N 36* 35' 54.347"	W 118* 6' 59.455"	N 36* 35.905783	W 118* 6.990916	400135	4050906
30	8	N 36.6026473*	W 118.1151306*	N 36* 36' 9.53"	W 118* 6' 54.47"	N 36* 36.15883'	W 118* 6.90783'	400264	4051373
30	9	N 36.6032982*	W 118.1142926*	N 36* 36' 11.874	W 118* 6' 51.453	N 36* 36.198	W 118* 06.855	400340	4051444
30	10	N 36.5992587*	W 118.1117338*	N 36* 35' 57.331"	W 118* 6' 42.242"	N 36* 35.955516'	W 118* 6.70403'	400564	4050993
30	11	N 36.5954558*	W 118.1153816*	N 36* 35' 43.641"	W 118* 6' 55.374"	N 36* 35.72735'	W 118* 6.9229'	400232	4050575
31	12	N 36.5832936*	W 118.1156751*	N 36* 34' 59.857"	W 118* 6' 56.43"	N 36* 34.997616'	W 118* 6.9405'	400191	4049226
31	13	N 36.584907*	W 118.113268*	N 36* 35' 5.665"	W 118* 6' 47.765"	N 36* 35.083	W 118* 06.885	400408	4049403
31	14	N 36.5828219*	W 118.1126013*	N 36* 34' 58.159"	W 118* 6' 45.365"	N 36* 34.96316'	W 118* 6.756083'	400465	4049171
31	15	N 36.5824428*	W 118.1130867*	N 36* 34' 56.974"	W 118* 6' 47.112"	N 36* 34.94656'	W 118* 6.7852'	400421	4049129
31	16	N 36.582305*	W 118.1117242*	N 36* 34' 56.298"	W 118* 6' 42.207"	N 36* 34.9383'	W 118* 6.70345'	400543	4049113
40	17	N 36.5993437*	W 118.1121697*	N 36* 35' 57.637"	W 118* 6' 43.811"	N 36* 35.960'	W 118.06.730'	400525	4051003
40	18	N 36.6000899*	W 118.1127544*	N 36* 36' .324"	W 118*6' 45.916"	N 36* 36.005'	W 118* 06.765'	400473	4051087
40	20	N 36.6015437*	W 118.114118*	N 36* 36' 5.557"	W 118* 6' 50.825"	N 36* 36.0926'	W 118* 6.84708'	400353	4051249
40	23	N 36.6026473*	W 118.1151306*	N 36* 36' 9.53"	W 118* 6' 54.47"	N 36* 36.15883'	W 118* 6.90783'	400264	4051373
40	27	N 36.6037806*	W 118.1188202*	N 36* 36' 13.61"	W 118* 7' 7.753"	N 36* 36.231	W 118* 07.122	399935	4051502
40	29	N 36.604344*	W 118.1176304*	N 36* 35' 15.638	W 118* 7' 3.469	N 36* 36.260	W 118* 07.060	400043	4051564
40	31	N 36.6032982*	W 118.1142926*	N 36* 36' 11.874	W 118* 6' 51.453	N 36* 36.198	W 118* 06.855	400340	4051444
40	35	N 36.6064078*	W 118.11808368*	N 36* 36' 23.068"	W 118* 7' 5.101"	N 36* 36.38446'	W 118* 07.08501'	400005	4051793
41	36	N 36.604344*	W 118.1176304*	N 36* 35' 15.638	W 118* 7' 3.469	N 36* 36.260	W 118* 07.060	400043	4051564
42	48	N 36.603998*	W 118.1169748*	N 36* 36' 14.393"	W 118* 7' 1.109"	N 36* 36.239883'	W 118* 7.018483'	400101	4051525
42	55	N 36.6041445*	W 118.1150664*	N 36* 36' 14.92"	W 118* 6' 54.239"	N 36* 36.2486'	W 118* 6.903983	400272	4051839
50	93	N 36.61050*	W 118.12913*	N 36* 36' 37.8"	W 118* 7' 44.9"	N 36* 36.630'	W 118* 7.748'	3999023	4052258
50	63	N 36.6026174*	W 118.1252583*	N 36* 36' 9.423"	W 118* 7' 41.73"	N 36* 36.15705	W 118* 7.6955	399090	4051383
50	69	N 36.61049*	W 118.12874*	N 36* 36' 37.8"	W 118* 7' 43.5"	N 36* 36.629'	W 118* 7.724'	399057	4052257
58	72	N 36.5966918*	W 118.0984783*	N 36* 35' 48.09"	W 118* 5' 54.4522"	N 36* 35.8015'	W 118* 5.9087'	401746	4050695
58	79	N 36.5974757*	W 118.0995459*	N 36* 35' 50.913"	W 118* 5' 58.635"	N 36* 35.84855'	W 118* 5.97275	401652	4050783
58	80	N 36.5974757*	W 118.0995459*	N 36* 35' 50.913"	W 118* 5' 58.635"	N 36* 35.84855'	W 118* 5.97275	401652	4050783
92	EXTRA 1	N 36.631702*	W 118.1221686*	N 36* 37' 54.127"	W 118* 7' 19.870"	N 36* 37.902'	W 118* 07.330'	399672	4054603
92	EXTRA 2	N 36.6305914*	W 118. 129219*	N 36* 37' 50.129	W 118* 7' 18.919	N 36* 37.835'	W 118* 7.315'	399693	4054479
93	EXTRA 3	N 36.6038742*	W 118. 1189248*	N 36* 13.947"	W 118* 7' 8.129"	N 36* 36.23245'	W 118* 7.135483	399926	4051513
93	EXTRA 4	N 36.6040799*	W 118.1171854*	N 36* 36' 14.688"	W 118* 7' 1.867"	N 36* 36.2448'	W 188* 7.031116'	400082	4051534
98	EXTRA 5	N 36.5958095*	W 118.1091653*	N 36* 35' 44.914"	W 118* 6' 32.995"	N 36* 35.74856'	W 118* 6.549916	400789	4050608

"quiet on the set"

It was Sunday evening, the end of the day, wrapping up the first Lone Pine Film Festival – twenty-five years ago – and Dad was driving from The Closing Campfire in the park to The Dow Villa Hotel and he said, "That was fun! I'm glad we got to do that." (He helped Kerry Powell put on the first Lone Pine Film Festival in 1990.) "Yep! Really glad we did that." You may recall, at the time, we didn't think it would be anything more than that: just that one year; just that celebration. Dad printed his new book and we'd had a wonderful weekend celebrating all the great movies made in those Alabama Hills. Mr. Roy Rogers himself joined us to unveil the Historical Marker at Whitney Portal & Movie Road! But to think it would be anything more than that? That The Festival would continue as long as – and as well as – it has? Well, that's because of both those initial volunteers and you.

Thank you for joining us in celebrating Where It Was Done, as we say. For coming up year after year to help continue the celebration. For coming up on your own throughout the year to go out and see those locations; and find new ones yourself! Indeed, as we wrap-up these first twenty-five years, we saw the passing of the torch. What Mom and Dad, Ray and Kerry and so many talented and generous people have made happen thus far has been amazing! What a delight that so many other wonderful people have taken that torch and carried it on!

From fans to come up with – and lead – new tours. To all the volunteers who freely give their time to share the movie making history. To the festival directors who lead the celebration. To the museum directors, particularly the current director, Bob Sigman, for his talents in presenting and protecting its assets. To The Board Of Directors, many of whom are lifetime members, for their dedication, foresight and work throughout each year to continue this commemoration. And for The Lone Pine Film History Museum that specifically – beautifully – showcases what The Festival and this book have championed thus far.

Because the real beauty of Lone Pine is its appeal to keep you coming back and celebrating that marvelous maze of boulders. That there are new faces ... yes, that can't help but be inspiring! How thrilling it is, still, after all these years, to be out there in those rocks and see people walking around with this book! After all, that's why Dad wrote it; to share that excitement, that discovery, with you.

And then Kerry said she wanted to put on a Festival to commemorate it all. Another great beginning! And you have more movies and stories and friends to share. Because they're still making movies out there! So it is – and continues to be – just the beginning.

The phrase "Quiet on The Set!" is two-fold. One, it's what The A.D. – Assistant Director – calls out at the beginning of a take, to get everyone quiet so cameras can roll. And, two, well ... at so many great shooting locations over the years – Iverson's, Corriganville, Melody Ranch; these Alabama Hills which really are the pinnacle – it's often, now, wonderfully quiet. Where you can get out into that Living Museum and relive those movie memories.

It is an honor to update this book.
It is a joy to share more movie history with you.

-- Melody Ogburn & Michael Holland
   September 2014

Michael Holland and sister Melody Holland-Ogburn represented their late father, Dave Holland, who published "On Location in Lone Pine," a pictorial guide to Hollywood's favorite movie locations for 95 years. (*10-16-14 Inyo Register*)

ex
(luding lists and quiz)

emy of Motion Picture Arts and Sciences 66
er, Jeanne 101
entures of Hajji Baba 76
ama Gates 12, 76, 83
ama Hills...82 and throughout!
no, The 10
no Village 10
idge, Kay 90
son, June 75
ng the Great Divide 17, 104
erican Cinematographer 66
ick, Rellis 24, 74, 75, 76, 78
hor Ranch 18, 20, 22, 23, 50, 101
horville 22, 23
erson, Earl 20
erson, Joy 20, 22, 23, 63
ie Oakley 17
che Rifles 10
uckle, Fatty 20, 21, 87, 101
y Girl 24, 102
az, Desi 16
gust, Joseph 66
ry, Gene 13, 15, 17, 28, 29, 41, 42, 49, 50, 58, 61, 62, 74, 75, 79

kground Rocks 18, 47, 49, 50, 87
d Day At Black Rock 20, 74
dger, Clarence 21
gdad 75
dwin, Alec 92
l, Lucille 16
rcroft, Roy, 99
r 20 20, 25, 49, 50, 63
r 20 Rides Again 30, 41, 58, 62
rton, Gregg 28
xter, Anne 13, 29
ale's Cut 10
ery, Wallace 101
ery Jr., Noah 42
hlmer, Rudy 66, 105
ngal Curve 30, 34, 40
nnett, Joan 76
rman, Pandro S. 68
ssie Brady 83, 84
eyond the Purple Hills 41
shop, 80, 84

Bishop, Mr. and Mrs. Samuel 84
Blackmer, Sidney 61
Blue Steel 28, 37
Boetticher, Budd 92, 93
Bogart, Humphrey 12, 13
Bogart Curve 18
Boles, John 18
Bonanza 26
Bonanza Family Restaurant 78
Bonnefin, Dorothy 74
Boots and Saddles 10, 11, 15, 42, 61, 62
Border Vigilantes 40, 58
Bow, Clara 98
Boyd, William 14, 19, 24, 25, 26, 41, 62, 101
Brady, James 84
Brigham Young 7, 14, 16, 23, 24, 48, 76
Briskin, Sam 68
Brodie, Steve 42
Bronson Canyon 10, 72
Brown, Ada 74, 75
Brown, George 74, 75
Brooks, Rand 25
Buchanan, Edgar 52, 62
Bunn, Lynne 78
Burnette, Smiley 3, 10, 15, 42, 61
Burson, Polly 76
Buttram, Pat 26, 41

C
California/Gabby Shack 30
Calistoga 22
Camp Independence 76, 80
Canutt, Yakima 24, 55, 58
Carrasco, Harold "Swede" 75, 77
Carrasco, Robbye 74, 75, 77
Carroll, Madeleine 73
Cartago 12, 83, 84, 85
Cassidy, Hopalong 17, 24, 37, 40, 42, 49, 50, 53, 58, 61, 62, 74, 101
Cattle Pocket 47, 50
Cederburg, Della 21, 74
Cerro Gordo 12, 18, 83, 84, 92
Charge of the Light Brigade 17, 47, 50, 61, 68
Charters, Spencer 13
Chesebro, George 99
Christenson, Clarence 18
Chrysler and Cook 23
Ciannelli, Eduardo 72
Cline, Roy 23, 24
Cline, Wilford 23

Clyde, Andy 25, 41, 58
Cody, Bill 61
Cody, Iron Eyes 42
Coffin, Tris 62
Colman, Ronald 73
Colt Comrades 62
Columbia Pictures 20, 22, 26
Comanche Station 34, 37
Comin' Round The Mountain 49, 50, 61, 62
Cooper, Gary 17, 26, 29, 34, 58, 61, 79, 86
Corrigan, Ray "Crash" 60
Corriganville 10, 17
Coso Mountains 82
Countz, Carl 74
Cow Town 41, 58, 61
Cowan, Jerome 13
Crosby, Bing 75
CSS Alabama 82, 83
Cuffe Guest Ranch 21
Cuffe, Irene 21
Curtis, Tony 50

D
Darnell, Linda 48
Dead End 13
Death Valley 12, 82
Dean, Eddie 101
Devil's Playground, The 42, 61
Diaz Lake 15, 76
Django Unchained 92
Dobie Gillis 33
Donat, Robert 73
Donner, Richard 91–92
Douglas, Kirk 104
Dow Hotel/Motel (Dow Villa) 74, 76, 78
Dow, G. Walter 78
Downey Jr., Robert 92
Duncan, Kenne 99
DWP 22

E
Earthquake (1872) 76, 85
Eastern California Museum 18, 21, 78, 83, 85
Eastwood, Clint 17, 26
Elam, Jack 13, 52, 62
Ellison, Jimmy 24
Estelle Mine 83
Evans, Dale 63
Evans, Madge 102

F
Fairbanks Sr., Douglas 21
Fairbanks Jr., Douglas 17, 31, 63, 65, 69

False Colors 42
Hands Across the Border 42, 61
Farr, Felicia 34
Fashball, Clarence 74
Favreau, Jon 92
Faylen, Frank 33
Ferguson, Perry 68
Ferguson's Landing 12, 84
Fiddlin' Buckaroo 37
Fisherman's Peak 80
Flores, Pablo 83
Flynn, Errol 17, 33, 34, 37, 47, 58, 61
Fonda, Henry 14
Fontaine, Joan 31, 63, 69, 73
Ford, Glenn 61
Ford, John 17, 69
Ford Point 10
Forman, Tom 101
Fort Independence 84
Foster, Preston 26, 102
Fox, 20th Century 14, 18, 20, 22, 25, 37, 47, 52, 76
Foxx, Jaime 92
Fremont, Captain John 83
French, Dr. Darwin 82
From Hell To Texas 22
Front Page, The 66
Frontier Days 61

G
Gable, Clark 68
Gallaher, Al 22
Gary Cooper Rock 18, 28, 29, 30, 34, 37, 40, 42, 48, 87
Gene Autry Rock 10, 11, 18, 30, 40, 42, 60, 61, 80
Gibson, Hoot 26, 50
Gifford, Frances 40
Gleason, James 25
Granger, Stewart 17
Grant, Cary 16, 17, 45, 63, 65, 69
Great Race, The 50
Great Western Savings 15
Grey, Zane 25, 37
Grill, The 78, 80
Guiol, Fred 68
Gunfighter, The 1, 17, 28, 89
Gunga Din 1, 5, 16, 18, 28, 30, 31, 45, 49, 50, 56, 58, 63, 64–73, 87, 92
Guns of Hate, 42
Gunsight Pass 58, 59, 73
Gunsmoke Ranch 42, 61

H
Haade, William 52
Hands Across the Border 42, 61
Hangman's Knot 33, 41
Hart, John 79
Hathaway, Henry 23
Have Gun, Will Travel 17
Hawks, Howard 66, 68
Hayden, Russell 19, 25, 101
Hayes, George "Gabby" 25, 28, 37, 53, 58, 63, 75
Hayward, Susan 52, 62
Hecht, Ben 66, 68
Henderson, Rudy 23, 75, 78
Henry, Bill 62
Heart of Arizona 49, 50, 62
High Plains Drifter 92
High Sierra 12, 13
Holland, Dave (rancher) 22
Holland, Holly 47
Holland, Michael 45, 92
Holloway, Sterling 62
Holt, Tim 10, 19, 26, 41, 42, 61, 79
Homer, Don and Alice 18
Hoodlums' Peak 82
Hop-A-Long Cassidy 24, 26
Hopalong Cassidy Productions 23
Hopalong Cassidy Enters 26
Hopalong Rides Again 62
Hoppy Cabin 14, 15, 21, 61, 62
Hoppy Rocks 40, 41, 42
How The West Was Won 10, 14, 23, 42, 49, 50, 61, 80, 104
Hoxie, Jack, 99

I
In Old Colorado 49
Independence 23, 78, 80, 83, 84
Indian Trading Post 33, 79, 85
Indian Agent 42
Ingram, Jack 99
Inyo Mountains 80
Iron Man 92
It's A Wonderful Life 33
Iverson's Movie Ranch 10, 17

J
Jaffe, Sam 45, 66, 69
Jagger, Dean 16, 22
Janes, Loren 49, 50
Joe Kidd 17, 26
Jolley, I. Stanford 99
Jones, Buck 17, 23, 76

Jory, Victor 50, 58, 63
Just Tony 22

K
Kane, Joe 3
Keeler 12
Kern River 21
Kim 33, 34, 37, 42, 58
King of the Khyber Rifles 16, 34, 37, 42, 74, 76
Kipling, Rudyard 66, 68
Knowles, Patric 17, 33
Korngold, Erick Wolfgang 73
Kortman, Robert 99
Kosla, Paul 26

L
La Florista Flower Shop 76
Lake Sherwood 10, 72
Langley, Chris 89, 92, 98
Lauten, Paul 15
Lauter, Harry 99
Law and Jake Wade 97
Law of the Pampas 19, 22, 24, 61
Light Brigade Rock 34, 40, 61
Lives of a Bengal Lancer 10, 23, 29, 34, 42, 48, 49, 61, 68, 87, 88
Livesey, Robert 73
Livingston, Bob 60
Little Lake 13
Lloyd's Western Wear 77
London, Tom 99
Lone Pine (name origin) 82
Lone Pine Campground 14
Lone Pine cemeteries 23, 76
Lone Pine Chamber of Commerce 26, 71
Lone Pine Creek 75, 82
Lone Pine Drugs 78
Lone Pine Film History Museum 93, 97, 106
Lone Pine Hotel 79
Lone Pine Peak 29, 80
Lone Pine Realty 74
Lone Ranger, the 60
Lone Ranger, The (1938) 30, 33, 55, 58
Lone Ranger, The (2013) 92
Lone Ranger, The (TV) 17, 26
Lone Ranger Ambush Site 18, 30, 33, 37, 40, 41, 61, 62
Lone Ranger Canyon 18, 33, 41
Lone Ranger Rock 10
Long Long Trailer, The 16

109

Los Angeles 22
Lucky Terror 50
Lucas Ranch 22
Lupino, Ida 13

M
MGM 20, 34, 66, 68
MacArthur, Charles 66, 68
MacDonald, Francis 41
Mahoney, Jock 61
Maltin, Leonard 98
Maps 12, 14-15, 30-31, 40-41, 42-43, 51, 58-59
Mapes, Ted 58
March, Fredric 92
Martin, Richard 26, 62
Marz Brothers 63
Maynard, Ken 17, 22, 26, 37, 82
McCollum, Ann-Marie 15
McElroy, Burl 74, 75
McGee, Bart and Alney 84
McKim, Sammy 60
McLaglen, Victor l7, 45, 65, 69
McQueen, Steve 102
Melody Ranch 29, 62
Merton, John 99
Michaels, Bill 85
Miss Brewster's Millions 21
Mitchum, Robert 25, 26, 49, 50, 62, 63
Mix, Tom 14, 20, 21, 22, 40, 54, 58, 76, 102
Moffatt Ranch 76
Mojave 21
Mojave Desert 83
Montana, Montie 101
Montgomery, George 47
Montgomery, Robert 68
Monument Valley 10
Molly Stevens 83, 84
Moore, Clayton 79
Moore, W.L. "Dad" 84
Morgan, Bruce 74, 78 .
Morris, Chester 22
Morris, Johnny 74
Mount Whitney 13, 80
Mount Whitney Cafe 74, 75
Movie Flats 7, 18, 65, 73, 76
Movie Road 3, 15, 17, 18, 29, 33, 53, 65, 76, 80
Mule Train 28, 40, 76
Mulford, Clarence E. 24, 25, 26
Murphy, Audie 10, 34
Murray, Don 22
Mysterious Desperado 61

N
Nadeau, Remi 83
Nevada 26
Nevada Smith 23, 83, 100
Newman, Alfred 73
Niven, David 17, 33
No, No, Nanette 21
Nonnand, Mabel 21
North To Alaska 14
Nyoka Cliff 10

O
Oak Creek Canyon 10
Oakie, Jack 69
Olancha l2, 68, 69, 74, 75, 82, 83, 84, 89
Old Tucson 10
Olivas, Ethel 45, 74, 75
Olivas, Henry 23, 24, 26, 74, 79
Olivas, Margaret 75
Olivas, Pete l5, 26, 50, 74, 75, 82, 101
Outing Magazine 24
Outlaws of the Desert 61
Owens, Richard 83
Owens Lake 12, 16, 83
Owens River 83
Owens Valley 16, 22, 82
Owens Valley Guide 85

P
Paiute Indians 61, 80, 85
Palance, Jack 79
Paramount Pictures 18, 20, 25
Passmore, Sheriff Thomas 84
Patterson, Mike 18, 83
Peck, Gregory 13, 17, 28, 29, 61, 89
Peckinpah, Sam 92
Peppard, George 104
Pidgeon, Walter 17
Pirates On Horseback 63
Plainsman and the Lady 40
Polyanna 92
Pot-sa-ga-wa Gardens 29, 40, 61, 62
Powell, Dick 74
Powell, Lee 55
Power, Tyrone 13, 16, 37, 42, 48, 76, 79
Preston, Robert 49, 50
Pride of the West 62
Putnam, Charles 84

R
Rainmaker, The 21
Range War 22, 101

Rawhide 18, 23, 30, 50, 52, 53, 62, 76, 80
Rawhide Burial Site 30, 49, 50, 61, 62
Red Dog 18,19, 30, 74, 98
Red Rock Canyon 10
Reed, Judge T.Y. 84
Reeves, George 25
Renaldo, Duncan 42, 61
Renegade Trail 25, 62
Republic Pictures 3, 20, 22, 26, 31, 61
Reynolds, Debbie 49, 50
Ride The High Country 92
Riders of the Purple Sage ('25) 14, 20, 21, 37, 40, 54, 58, 76
Riders of the Purple Sage ('41) 47, 50
Ridin' Kid From Powder River 26
RKO 5, 10, 20, 26, 54, 63, 65, 68, 72, 73
Roach, Hal 68
Robbs, Allie 23
Roberson, Chuck 58
Robinson, Edward G. 79
Rockwell, Jack 3
Rogers, Roy 3, 16, 26, 42, 61, 74 ,75, 86
Rogers, Will 21
Rootin' Tootin" Rhythm 58
Roundup, The 20, 2l, 101
Royer, Mike 11
Ruiz Hill 28, 54-59, 73, 75, 77
Ryan, Robert 20
Ryan, Sheila 26

S
Sabu 73
Sand dunes...see Olancha
Sayre, Joel 68
Schildkraut, Joseph 62
Schumacher, Genny 13, 28, 85
Scott, Randolph 23, 26, 33, 53, 61, 74, 104
Seasons Restaurant 78, 80
Seidel, Tom 42
Sets 14, 15, 18, 19, 20, 21, 22, 28, 30, 31, 36, 38, 40, 45, 49, 50, 52, 53, 54, 58, 59, 61, 62, 63, 64, 66, 67, 68, 71, 72, 74, 85, 90, 101
Sharpe, David 69
Sheffield, Johnny 12, 68
Sheffield, Reginald 68
Shelton, Bill 45

Secrets of the Wasteland 37
Selander, Lesley 101
Seven Men From Now 53
Shannon, Harry 58
Sherman, Harry 25, 26, 101
Shooting of Dan McGrew 21
Shultz, George and Hazel 18, 82
Sierra Cafe 74
Silent Conflict 41, 62
Silverheels, Jay 79
Skull Rock 55, 58
Small, Edward 66
Smith, Jedediah 83
Soldiers Three 17
Song of Texas 58
Song of the West 18, 85, 86
Spainhower, Jeanne 63
Spainhower, Russ 18, 20, 22, 23, 54, 58, 76, 101
Spanish Garden 78
Springfield Rifle 23, 26, 61
Stagecoach 10
Stagecoach Kid 41, 61
Stanwyck, Barbara 79
Star is Born, A 92
Star Trek V 18
Starrett, Charles 26
Stevens, George 5, 65, 68, 72, 73
Stevens, Colonel Sherman 84
Stewart, Jodi 18, 83
Stewart, Peggy 33, 62
Stockman, Boyd 28
Superman 25
Sutherland, Eddie 101
Swansea 83

T
Taliaferro, Hal 58
Tantrapur Village 18, 45, 50, 65
Tarantino, Quentin 92
Tarzan's Desert Mystery 12, 75

Taylor, Ken 11
Teal, Ray 99
Temple, Shirley 17
Temple of Kali 31, 65, 72
Tent city (Gunga Din) 30, 65, 66, 71
Terhune, Max 52, 60
Terror Trail 103
Thalberg, Irving 66
Three Faces West 92
Three Men From Texas 58
Three Mesquiteers 42, 52, 60, 61
Three On The Trail 49
Three Passes 37, 40, 41
Thundercloud, Chief 18
Tone, Franchot 17, 34, 68
Tracy, Spencer 20, 68
Trail to San Antone 33, 62
Turner, George A. 66
Tuttle Creek 82
Tuttle Creek Road 15, 16, 21, 61, 62,87
Tycoon 54, 58, 74

U
Under Western Stars 3, 8
Universal Pictures 20
USC 13

V
Van Dyke, Reuben 23
Vasquez, Tiburcio 80, 84
Vasquez Rocks 10, 85
Violent Men 61
Visitor Center, Interagency 12 83

W
Walker, Joseph 82, 83
Wanger, Walter 76
Warner Brothers 18, 20, 26

Wagons Westward 22, 23
Waltz, Christoph 92
Water Water Everywhere 21
Waterhole No. 3 12
Wayne, John 10,15, 23, 28, 30, 31, 37, 54, 58, 62
Wee Willie Winkie 17
Weismuller, Johnny 12
West of the Pecos 26,62
Western Frontier 61
Westward Ho l, 23, 30, 31, 37, 61, 62
Whiting, LaVeme 76
Whitney, Josiah 80
Whitney Portal 13
Whitney Portal Road 16, 18, 21, 30, 54, 37
Wild Bill Hickok 26
Widmark, Richard 13
Wilde, Lois 62
Willey, Jeanne 78
Williams, Guinn "Big Boy" 42, 61, 76
Williams, Jack 49, 50
Winnedumah Hotel 78
Wishbone, the 29
Withers, Grant 63
Witney, William 55, 92
Wood, Britt 101
Wood, Natalie 50
Woods, Harry 97
Worth, Harry 62
Wyeth, N.C. 24
Wynn, Keenan 50

Y
Yellow Sky 18, 28, 29, 30, 38, 39, 40, 74, 80, 88
Yosemite Valley 83
Yrigoyen, Joe 17, 33, 62

You've just been on location in Lone Pine.

Hurry back.
The rocks and the memories will always be waiting for you.